# MIXT

## SALADS

# A CHEF'S BOLD CREATIONS

# MIXT

## SALADS

TEN SPEED PRESS
Berkeley

**ANDREW SWALLOW** *with* ANN VOLKWEIN

Some of the recipes in this book include raw eggs, meat, or fish. When these foods are consumed raw, there is always the risk that bacteria, which are killed by proper cooking, may be present. For this reason, when serving these foods raw, always buy certified salmonella-free eggs and the freshest meat and fish available from a reliable grocer, storing them in the refrigerator until they are served. Because of the health risks associated with the consumption of bacteria that can be present in raw eggs, meat, and fish, these foods should not be consumed by infants, small children, pregnant women, the elderly, or any persons who may be immunocompromised.

Copyright © 2010 by Andrew Swallow
Photographs copyright © 2010 by Sara Remington

All rights reserved.
Published in the United States by Ten Speed Press, an imprint of the Crown Publishing Group,
a division of Random House, Inc., New York.
www.crownpublishing.com
www.tenspeed.com

Ten Speed Press and the Ten Speed Press colophon are registered trademarks of Random House, Inc.

Eco-gourmet is a registered trademark of Mixt Greens.

Library of Congress Cataloging-in-Publication Data is on file with the publisher.

ISBN 978-1-58008-057-6

Printed in China

This book has been printed on paper sourced in accordance with sustainable forest management.

Design by Ed Anderson and Colleen Cain

Many thanks to our excellent photography team including Sara Remington, Nani Steele,
and Ethel Brennan.

10 9 8 7 6 5 4 3 2 1

First Edition

This is for you, mom—
thanks for believing in me.

# CONTENTS

# INTRODUCTION

In the great city of San Francisco, home to the most obsessive foodies in the United States, I've created salad junkies who are just as passionate as the original coffee junkies. I'll stop by any of my Mixt Greens restaurants in the middle of the afternoon and there's always a line out the door. It makes me feel good to see all those people eating those wonderful greens. One day a man walked up to me and said, "I don't know how you did it, but you've even gotten *men* to eat salad all the time!" Now, granted, they're not eating prewashed greens thrown into a bowl and loaded up with some overly sugared dressing . . . These are my kinds of salads: organic, hyper-fresh, deeply layered with flavors and textures, and totally, completely addictive.

Cooking with fine products and the conscious use of seasonal ingredients have been part of my cooking vocabulary for a long time, starting on the East Coast. After a stint at New York's Gramercy Tavern, I attended the Culinary Institute of America. While there, I studied Alice Waters's farm-to-table movement, which supported local, organic, and sustainable eating. I could hear California calling. New York is a food mecca, but it is more French influenced, while the farm-to-table chefs in California have more of a fusion-influenced cuisine that was exciting to me. And when I eventually came to San Francisco, I could see that the food economy was really driven by local artisans. Farmers deliver directly to restaurants here. The interaction is huge, and the community is highly aware of local, sustainable eating. It's Alice Waters's legacy in full force. So, after working in various restaurants, I was convinced this was the place I wanted to start my own restaurants. To be embraced by this highly evolved—and picky—super-foodie community would be a great feeling, and the San Francisco equivalent of "If you can make it here . . . ." A gig at Gary Danko ended up being the key step in becoming friendly with the city.

After all, part of the reason I created Mixt Greens was to give to this community—to deliver premium, good food in a fast-casual environment. To create fun, accessible fine dining that's not intimidating. And, in the process, to teach people how to eat in a sustainable way.

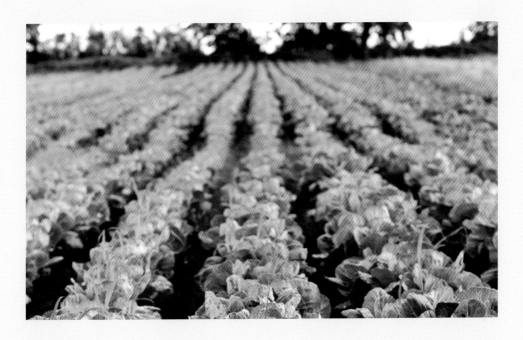

# LIVING RESPONSIBLY

Along the way, I've adopted habits that lower my personal environmental impact. Here's a rundown of some commonsense, sustainability basics for your kitchen:

- Buy local products and produce.
- Eat and cook seasonal foods.
- Use wooden tools in the kitchen, but never use wooden salad bowls. They look good and are environmentally friendly but the oils and vinegars leach into the wood and make it taste bad, whereas there are no remnants in stainless steel bowls. Think of it like this: wine that's aged in porous wooden barrels has an earthy taste of the wood; wine that's aged in stainless steel barrels has a cleaner mineral or fruity finish.
- Use dishrags, not paper towels, and cloth napkins instead of paper.
- Eliminate the use of disposable utensils and plates.
- Recycle, and instead of lining the recycling bin with a bag you buy in a grocery store, use a paper bag your grocery store packs your items in—then you've recycled that, too.
- Use green cleaning products, including a green hand soap. This is really important, because chemicals on your hands can transfer to your food!
- Composting at home is very easy if you don't have a commercial service. If you can garden as well, create compost to fertilize your garden. (For non-gardeners, there are a lot of easy things to grow, from a windowsill herb garden to a pot of tomatoes on your back step—now, that's local.)
- Know what you're going to get out of your refrigerator before you open it. Each time you open the fridge you're using tremendous energy, including the cooling and even the lightbulb that turns on. Know where your item is and grab as many things as possible at once.
- When buying new appliances, look for the highest ENERGY STAR rating.
- When selecting your foods, choose unprocessed, fresh ingredients, fresh vegetables, fresh everything. A tip: when in the supermarket, keep to the perimeter. Stay out of the middle. You want fresh meat, fish, produce, and dairy, not packaged items. Avoid the frozen food section. Buying processed food is outrageously expensive, and there are extra calories to boot. Make it fresh!
- When buying produce, check out the numbers on the labels to know how it was grown (more on that in the first chapter).

# BIRTH OF MIXT GREENS

When I was sixteen, I started working at the local Chatham Sandwich Shop in my New Jersey hometown. At that point I never expected that I would make a career out of it. At twenty, I started working in fine dining and I got hooked. But the one thing that always drove me nuts was the lifestyle: coming home at 2 a.m., sleeping 'till noon, then starting all over again the next day—plus having to work weekends and holidays. This all got me thinking about how I could improve my routine while working in this industry that I care so deeply about.

Then it came to me: open a high-end, quick-service restaurant using all that I learned in top-notch gourmet restaurants over the years. I got excited rethinking the whole approach to fast-casual food—creating a chef driven company serving the highest quality local and organic ingredients, all with the highest level attention to customer service. It sounded like a fantastic idea; I knew I wanted to share my passion for food with the masses. I had been playing around with a few potential concepts when one day my best friend Joanne suggested salads. Man, did that get the wheels turning. While driving back from snowboarding in Lake Tahoe with my sister and my brother-in-law, I turned to them and said, "What do you guys think about a salad concept?" With that, the collaboration began.

With the expertise of my sister, who has a degree in biodiversity, conservation, and management, and the business savvy of my brother-in-law, a partnership was born. On first glance, it seemed crazy; family members are the last people I ever expected to found a restaurant with. But man, what a great call—we're a dynamic trio and every day is full of adventure. We're happy to say that Mixt Greens is not just great food with a side of environmental responsibility—it's the whole experience.

# THE SEASONAL TABLE

# WHY EAT SEASONAL?

Befriend your local organic farmers. You'll find the friendship becomes a lesson in patience and variety that illustrates how working with the seasons, organic products, and sustainable harvesting gives you the most wonderful flavors and the best quality of life. When seasons change, it's like Christmas for me. There's nothing like biting into sweet white corn in the summertime or tasting a wonderfully sweet, yet acidic, blood orange in the winter. The anticipation I've had all year makes them that much more satisfying and exciting to devour when they first appear at the market. I even daydream about next season's produce, getting ready to try out some new ideas. I've put together a seasonal chart for you to follow that will help you prepare salads, and the rest of your meals, too. Use the chart to buy foods at their peak harvesting time, when they're at their most flavorful and abundant at the market. If you adopt this way of eating, you'll see that, as the adage goes, good things come to those who wait. Seasonal eating is a celebration of the earth's wonderful nutrients, and seasonal and sustainable eating go hand in hand, because when you support your local economy by eating what's in season and buying from your farmers' markets, you're eating in a sustainable way. So leave the box food stores in the dust—the products they sell have little to no flavor. Just think, back in the day you would go to a specific place to buy your produce and they knew you by name; you'd have a personal relationship with the butcher, and you'd trust the products he was selling to you and your family. We need to support small community purveyors so we can have those relationships again. If you don't have a local farmers' market, your next best options are small local specialty markets or Whole Foods.

You're on the hunt for what I call feel-good food, or eating from the roots. When you know where and how something is produced, it makes you feel better about consuming it. That's also called "clean food." Eating things that have been sprayed with pesticides is not good for your body, so shell out the extra money if you can get organic. The more we support our local economies, the better products those economies will produce for us. In San Francisco, I've seen the farmers' market reach maximum capacity with local farms and artisans. They're very well supported in the Bay Area, and it's plain to see they *like* to produce these wonderful products for their community. And there's always someone growing or making something new for the community to try, which is a very exciting thing if you have a passion for food and your local area. My cooking philosophy is to cook simple and from the heart. I get so much enjoyment out of cooking small, intimate dinners for friends and family. Cooking simply is very easy: just let the food speak for itself, and don't overdo the number of ingredients. For example, just slice a few varieties of heirloom Early Girl tomatoes, place them on a plate, drizzle with a fine olive oil, and sprinkle with sea salt and cracked pepper. It does not get much better than that in summertime; it's like the Fourth of July in your mouth. That's the look I want to see when I watch my friends eat my food. They enjoy it as much as I enjoy going to the farmers' market and choosing, creating, and preparing.

There is an art to tossing a good salad, mixing the proper amount of textures together matched with the right acid and oil and seasoned well. I can always tell how well a kitchen is run and whether there is a chef on "the pass" if I get a perfectly dressed salad. Nine times out of ten, when I order a salad at a restaurant, it's overdressed. Why? No one ever cares about the salad tosser; chefs are more worried about their signature dishes. I don't get it—why put something on your menu just for filler? It's a wasted opportunity. It's starting to change, but most chefs are still more passionate about their foie gras dishes, which is very funny to me because they all pretty much taste the same. So move on, people, there's so much more you can do with a salad, and it's not going to clog your arteries. My goal is to show you just how incredible the overlooked salad can be.

## PRODUCE SHOPPING: IT'S A NUMBERS GAME

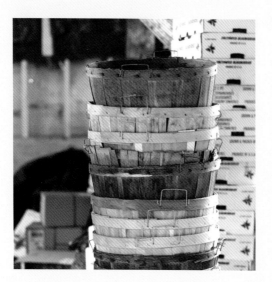

Whether you're at a neighborhood market, Whole Foods, or a small specialty store, there may not always be a sign to tell you where or how an item was grown, but there's always a number assigned. When it starts with a 4, it is conventionally grown. But beware: although this special code exists, most producers realize that the majority of consumers are trying to steer clear of genetically modified foods—so they've stopped using the separate designation. The number you want is 9, which means organic—not altered by a scientist or sprayed with pesticides. Organic produce will not always look the prettiest, but it will always taste much better and be much healthier.

# SEASONAL PRODUCE CHART

Get in tune with the seasons and capture peak flavor. This chart makes it easy to uncover when produce is at its prime, with a reference to the appropriate recipes in the book. Check out the supremely edible gifts of the season.

## SPRING

| | |
|---|---|
| Apricots | May–July |
| Artichokes | March–May |
| Asparagus | March–June |
| Blueberries | May–July |
| Green Garlic | February–June |
| Fava Beans | February–July |
| Leeks | March–June |
| Fennel | February–June |
| Morel Mushrooms | April–June/July |
| Pea Shoots | February–June |
| Radish | April–June |
| Strawberries | February–September |
| Watercress | April–June |

## SUMMER

| | |
|---|---|
| Blackberries | May–July |
| Eggplant | July–October |
| Figs | June–October |
| Bean Varieties | July–November |
| Lemon Cucumber | July–September |
| Lychee | June–August |
| Melons | July–September |
| Nectarines | June–October |
| Pear | July–September |
| Peaches | June–September |
| Sweet Corn | July–September |
| SummerPeppers | July–September |
| Summer Squash | June–September |
| Tomatoes | June–October |
| Watermelon | June–October |

## FALL

| | |
|---|---|
| Apples | July–November |
| Asian Pear | September–November |
| Butternut | August–January |
| Belgian Endive | Year round |
| Brussels Sprouts | September–May |
| Grape Varieties | July–October |
| Parsnip | October–April |
| Rutabaga | October–April |
| Chanterelles | September–February |
| Persimmons | October–January |
| Pomegranate | September–January |
| Turnip | September–April |

## WINTER

| | |
|---|---|
| Beets | Year round |
| Castlefranco | December–March |
| Cabbage | Year round |
| Green Papaya | Year round |
| Grapefruit | November–March |
| Blood Orange | December–March |
| Cara Cara Orange | November–March |
| Fingerling Potato | Year round |
| Jicama | Year round |
| Radicchio | November–March |
| Tangerines | November–March |
| Passion Fruit | Year round |
| Mango | Year round |
| Pineapple | Year round |
| Meyer Lemon | October–April |

# BUILDING A SALAD

I call my recipe-creation process "building" a salad because I use identifiable, simple techniques that will help you expertly balance flavors and textures to make your own creations. Once you know the profiles of the seasonal ingredients and how they interact, it's easy to choose the right produce, meats, and dressings. The first things I think about are which part of the season I'm in, what's available, and what profile of salad I want to create. Do I want an appetizer-style salad or a light entrée-style salad, or a more robust second course? I consider the type of event, too, whether it is an intimate dinner with family, a large gathering of friends, or something at the restaurant. Next, I break down what I'm going to make. Appetizer salads depend on the second course. If it's springtime and I'm serving spring lamb as a main course, I would want a light and fresh salad instead of heavier flavors. I might use fava beans with pecorino, herbs, and lemon. But an entrée salad for spring could incorporate lamb in the salad itself. A lamb main-dish salad could have spring lamb, seasonal fava beans, perhaps wild ramps, and olives. Or perhaps an olive tapenade vinaigrette. It's all about thinking of the classic flavors and accompaniments that complement the protein, or produce, I've selected. Try to balance rich, salty, bitter, sweet, and tangy flavors in concert with one another.

While you're picking the elements of the salad, pay attention to texture. Just as with the flavor elements, you want a variety of textures. If you have all soft ingredients with soft lettuce, you're just going to have a bowl of mush. Try to have crisp, crunchy, creamy, and chewy textures represented for an ideal "mouthfeel." That may sound strange, but it adds hugely to the experience of the recipe. For example, nuts have one of the strongest crunchy textures and cheeses have one of the softest and creamiest, therefore they complement one another. Grapes are chewy and sweet. Apples are crisp. With those four ingredients, I've got crunchy, creamy, chewy, and crisp, so there's a foundation of different textures to blend together for a balanced final product. Try to have one in each category if you can find seasonal ingredients that work together. When looking for the best lettuce, think about both the flavor and the texture. Lettuce can be bitter, buttery, sweet, earthy, tart, spicy, silky soft, crunchy, or chewy (yes, chewy, like chicory). For example, radicchio is crunchy and so bitter it almost burns your mouth. Check out my "Types of Greens" section on page 21 if this feels intimidating. Too often, the ubiquitous mesclun is used, which can be perfect, but sometimes another lettuce might make the salad sing!

The acids and seasonings in the sauce or vinaigrette are what pull it all together once you've designed your protein and produce components. Think about complementary flavors when constructing the dressing. A lot of my recipes use more than one vinegar or oil. I'll use a percentage of grapeseed oil cut with olive oil, or straight canola oil, or canola oil and olive oil. When it's a vinaigrette base that uses a good extra virgin olive oil, you don't want the flavors to completely overpower the oil. A combination of Meyer lemon juice, shallots, extra virgin olive oil, and a little salt and black pepper is one of my favorites. They work so well together because you can taste the Meyer lemon as well as the olive oil—good olive oil you want to taste, not waste. If you're looking for a clean, neutral taste, use grapeseed and canola oils. Mustard, interestingly, tastes great with chicken, pork, and fish, but not steak. Balsamic does not work with fish, and balsamic with pork is a little too much because pork is so sweet on its own. However, when you combine red wine vinegar, which is really tart, with a little balsamic, it totally works with pork.

## ANATOMY OF A SALAD: THE CATCH

When putting together the salad The Catch for Mixt Greens, I first thought, "What tastes best with salmon in wintertime?" Citrus. You've got the smokiness and fattiness of salmon, which needs to be cut by something that is bitter and sweet, so I added shallots to the citrus; something salty would complement it, so I added capers. But it needed a flavor infusion, so I came up with the intense combo of tarragon and dill. Those herbs enhance all of it. Next, I added watermelon radishes, which are earthy with a little bit of heat and spiciness to them. For the lettuce, a delicate, crunchy mixed greens wasn't going to work. I wanted something rich, not bitter, and creamy, because salmon is creamy. Romaine would be too watery—but butter lettuce hit the right note. Next came the vinaigrette. What would I want to drink with salmon? Champagne, not wine or sherry. So I created a complementary, high-acid champagne-vinegar vinaigrette that breaks down the fattiness of the salmon and can stand up to the rest of the flavor components.

It's just a matter of thinking it through, step by step. With steak, I might use blue cheese, caramelized onions, and potatoes, and a deep, rich balsamic dressing. And all of that goes beautifully with red leaf lettuce that has a neutral, earthy flavor and good texture. The bottom line is, don't be afraid to use ingredients that you'd never think to make a salad out of. It's simple if you just focus on two things: a variety of seasonal flavors that taste great together and that have textural variation. To make this all even easier, I've pulled together some basic guides to lettuce, meats, seafood, herbs and seasonings, and oils and vinegars. These guides, in concert with the seasonal produce chart (page 14), can be your Salad Blueprint. Now, get building!

## SHOPPING FOR GREENS

I like to shop for my seasonal greens at my farmers' market, and I've noticed as people have become more conscious about what they put into their bodies the demand for more varieties of greens has increased—and the farmers have enthusiastically responded. You can see the passion they put into growing their lettuces, and the excitement they feel when introducing new varieties to their customers. Everybody has their staple favorites, but the range can be anywhere from delicate and buttery to extremely bitter and chewy.

If you can't get to the farmers' market, always buy the loose greens that are on display, they tend to be fresher. The prepackaged greens at the grocery store have often been gassed so that they'll hold for long periods of time.

One of the things people like most about salads is the crunchy texture, so once you've got your greens home heed these storage tips to keep them crisp:

- Keep greens in the refrigerator, wrapped in a slightly moist towel, or if your leaves are loose, in a bowl in the refrigerator with a moist towel on top.
- Be sure to clean your lettuce well—not to rinse off the pesticides because I know you're buying organic (right?), but to remove the little critters and the tiny pieces of grit that hide out toward the core. A great tool is the salad spinner, which removes the excess water from the greens without extra bruising. If you don't have one, make sure you pat the greens dry before serving; excess water dilutes the flavor in the salad, an awful crime.
- To eliminate as much wilting as possible, wash and dry your lettuce, and wait until you're just about to plate or toss before tearing the leaves apart.

Bottom line, try some new varieties and take good care of your greens and you'll reap the rewards in your salads.

# Types of Greens

**Baby Spinach** Soft and tender in texture, baby spinach has a mild, clean flavor—not bitter or astringent like fully matured spinach. Try it with berry salads.

**Belgian Endive** With its bitter juicy spears and tangy flavor, endive is a wonderful choice. Add it to green salads for a contrast in color, texture, and flavor. Choose the small, light, crisp hearts to maximize the flavor. I love it paired with goat cheese and pears.

**Butter** Also known as Bibb or Boston, butter lettuce is delicate in flavor with a velvety texture. Hands down, it's the most popular lettuce at Mixt Greens—and it's my favorite lettuce, too. People love its creamy, buttery flavor; I suggest using this lettuce with citrus.

**Iceberg** Also known as crisphead, this lettuce is, well, crisp, like its name, and it has the mildest flavor of all the lettuces. It has a light green color with firm leaves. Crisphead is all about the crunchy texture, not the flavor. I think it's best quartered and topped with a rich blue cheese dressing.

**Frisée** This member of the chicory family has a blanched white center with tender, feathery leaves that pack a bittersweet flavor punch. When selecting, make sure you look for firm leaves. They're always a little tan at the base, and go from yellow or white into the delicate greens. Try it with crispy pork belly and a poached egg . . . mmmm.

**Mâche** Also called lamb's lettuce, mâche is a tiny, dark green plant with a soft, buttery, and nutty flavor. It has a fragile structure, so gently toss and serve it immediately so that the leaves do not wilt prematurely. This green should be used the day it is bought. I like to serve it with roasted baby beets and toasted hazelnuts.

**Little Gems** This lettuce is often described as a combination of butter lettuce and romaine. It's crisp and juicy, like romaine, and soft and sweet, like butter. The nutty flavor has a reserved sweetness that I guarantee you'll enjoy.

**Mesclun Mix** Typically, this is a light, fresh blend of lettuce leaves with a mix of soft and spicy greens. Sometimes radicchio and frisée are mixed in to give it more body and a stronger flavor.

**Pea Sprouts** These tendrils plus the uppermost leaves are one of the secrets to be discovered in Asian cooking. The fresh, crunchy texture is bursting with a distinct pea flavor. They're great to used on their own or thrown in a mesclun mix.

**Radicchio** There are four varieties of radicchio: Castelfranco, Verona, Treviso, and Chioggia (which is the most common type). All have a flavor that is a bit bitter and mildly peppery with a chewy and crunchy texture—except Castelfranco, which has a mild flavor and lettuce-like texture. Mix it with softer or mild-tasting greens for variety.

**Red Leaf** Also known as looseleaf, this lettuce has beautiful red-tipped leaves. Its soft, mild flavor works wonderfully on its own or mixed with stronger-flavored greens.

**Rocket** Also called arugula, rocket is in the mustard family. It has a tender leaf with a peppery taste and sharp, bitter bite. Rocket is great on its own or in a mix. It pairs well with salty, rich, sweet, and acidic ingredients. Look for baby rocket, which has a softer texture and milder flavor. Rocket is best in the spring and fall. This is one of my favorite lettuces for salads—and one of my top garnishes for other dishes.

**Romaine** This lettuce is known for its fresh, sweet, slightly bitter flavor and crisp, firm texture. The outer leaves are much darker in color, and the lighter-colored hearts tend to have a stronger tartness. Classically paired with Caesar salad, romaine is a utilitarian lettuce that can pretty much stand up to anything you ever toss it with. Look for speckled romaine for its beautiful color.

**Watercress** This pungent member of the mustard family has a peppery, tangy punch and a slight juiciness. It's great on its own and tastes great mixed with chicories. Because it's delicate and highly perishable, make sure you use it the day it is purchased. Look for a bright green color with no yellow and a fresh smell.

## LETTUCE FLAVOR PROFILES IN BRIEF

**Mild:** Baby Spinach, Butter, Crisphead, Lamb's Lettuce, Little Gems, Mesclun Mix, Pea Shoots, Red Leaf, Romaine

**Tart:** Belgian Endive, Frisée, Hearts of Romaine, Watercress

**Bitter:** Radicchio, Rocket

# SHOPPING FOR MEATS

The best places to buy meats are your local butcher shop or farm stand where you can ask lots of questions. Shopping for meat at a box food store is very difficult, because the label usually only tells you the grade and cut and maybe the breed. Ask your butcher where the meat comes from and how the animal was cared for. It's really important to buy Certified Humane, which allows the animal to engage in its natural behaviors; such animals are raised with a sufficient amount of space, shelter, and gentle handling to limit stress, and have fresh water and a healthy diet without antibiotics or hormones. Stay away from factory-farmed poultry. These chickens are raised in an inhumane manner and are pretty much tasteless. Look for cage-free or free-range poultry, and if you don't have to sell your soul to meet the price, buy organic. Beef should have a deep-red color and look dry but shiny.

# CATTLE BREEDS

**American Kobe:** It's very common to find American Kobe products on the menus of higher-end restaurants. It comes from original genetic lines of Wagyu cattle from Japan.

**Angus:** There is "red" and "black;" look for Certified Angus, which is the best Black Angus.

**Wagyu:** This includes many different breeds. Wagyu beef is known for its wonderful marbling of fat and is extremely tender.

# BUTCHER TALK: BEEF TERMS

**Certified Humane:** Animals have freedom to move, and antibiotics and artifical means to induce growth are prohibited.

**Certified Organic:** Cattle raised on vegetarian feed grown without chemical pesticides and fertilizers.

**Natural:** Beef that does not contain artificial ingredients.

**Prime:** The highest grade for American beef.

**Wet versus Dry Aging:** Aging beef gives it a slight gamy flavor and also increases tenderness. Wet-aged beef is vacuum-sealed and aged. Dry-aged beef is hung in a cold, moderately humid place to tenderize it and concentrate the flavor.

## Types of Beef for Salads

**Filet Mignon** The filet mignon is considered to be the most tender cut of beef, and the most expensive, but in my opinion, it lacks flavor. However, if you get American Kobe or Japanese Wagyu filet mignon, both of which have significant fat content, the high-end reputation fits the flavor. It's best served rare to medium-rare to achieve maximum tenderness.

**Flat Iron** Also called top blade, flat iron steak usually has a significant amount of marbling that gives it a wonderful flavor and juiciness. Thinly sliced, it works great on top of salads. It's a thin cut of meat, so it cooks very fast. You don't want to cook it much more than medium-rare or you'll lose the juiciness. It also takes quick marinades well.

**Hanger** This cut is the best-kept secret of steak lovers. Hanger is prized for its full flavor. The meat is not particularly tender, so make sure you cook it quickly at high heat, because it's best served rare or medium-rare to avoid toughness. It's sometimes known as "butcher's steak" because butchers would often keep it for themselves rather than offer it for sale.

**Strip Steak** This is one of the highest-quality cuts, with great marbling and that classic "steak" flavor. Cook it at a high heat to crisp the outside, and then bring it down to a slow roast. Cook rare to medium-rare. I like these steaks to be cut 2 inches thick, and then I thinly slice the cooked meat and place it on top of a salad.

## Types of Poultry for Salads

**Chicken** What is there to say about chicken? It is the most popular meat we serve at Mixt Greens. Almose everyone loves to eat chicken. Chicken breast works best for salads because it's easy to cook and requires little labor. It's a healthy option as well, because chicken breast has very little fat.

**Duck** I like to use duck in two ways in a salad: duck breast and confit. Duck breast has a wonderful, succulent, gamy flavor with a crispy skin that chicken lacks. I like to thinly slice it and top a salad with it. Duck confit on salad is an almost perfect marriage. The rich, fatty, salty flavor pairs perfectly with vinegar and oil.

## Types of Pork for Salads

**Bacon** There's not too much to say about pork belly. It just makes everything taste better. Just be sure you buy a natural product when you use bacon. (Let's face it: it's already bad enough for you.)

**Chorizo** There are many different styles of this highly seasoned ground pork sausage, and it comes either fresh or dried. I prefer Spanish and Mexican styles. Although most people would probably not think of putting chorizo in a salad, when matched up with the right ingredients, it does wonders. Think dates, tomato, and peppers, and take it from there.

**Pancetta** This salt-cured and spiced pork belly from Italy is not smoked. It usually comes in sausage-shaped rolls, and it's great to use in place of bacon because it tends to be on the salty side.

**Pork Tenderloin** This is the filet mignon of the pig, and it has a super-tender texture. I recommend a marinade or a rub because the tenderloin has a mild flavor. Try to find Berkshire pork when using pork products. It is full in flavor and renowned for its superb meat marbling.

**Prosciutto** My favorite style of this dried, cured Italian ham is *prosciutto di Parma,* sliced paper-thin. I think it's best paired with fresh mozzarella, figs, and fresh melon.

## Types of Lamb for Salads

**Lamb Tenderloin, Sirloin, and Loin** I like to use a couple of different cuts of lamb on salad, including these three. I recommend marinating them in extra virgin olive oil, fresh garlic, and rosemary. All three cuts are full in flavor and tender, and best served medium-rare.

## SHOPPING FOR SEAFOOD

The most important thing to remember when buying seafood is to use a reputable store or fishmonger. Then, ask the right questions. When did they receive the product? Is it fresh or previously frozen? Wild caught or farm raised? Where did the product come from? If you're landlocked, most likely the fish has been previously frozen—no matter what the sign may say—unless it's a store that specializes in fresh seafood. Most fish have seasons, which you should try to follow. Just ask. You'll also save money on a product when it's in season because the markets will be flooded with them. When choosing your seafood, there are a couple of steps to follow. Ask the purveyor to hand the fish over on a piece of deli paper. Look to make sure it's nice and firm, with a shiny flesh. Look for any discoloration. Smell the fish, and if it does not smell like the ocean, hand it back.

## Types of Seafood for Salads

**Albacore Tuna** "White meat" tuna has a couple of different names, including tombo and albacore. It has a creamy flesh that tastes buttery. When shopping for tombo, look for a pinkish color. It does well poached, seared, or raw, but if you're going to eat it raw specify sushi-grade tuna. Again, buy troll- or pole-caught tuna; just ask your fishmonger how it was caught.

**Arctic Char** This fish is in the salmon and trout family. It has delicate red flesh with a firm texture and a mild, clean taste. When grilling or roasting, cook it to medium-rare for the best results. Be sure to buy closed farmed fish, which means the fish is separated from the external environment.

**Crab** This crustacean has a delicate texture with a sweet, mild taste. Depending on where you live, fresh lump blue and fresh Dungeness are both great on salads. Their spongy texture picks up other flavors beautifully.

**Diver Scallops** These bivalves have a meaty, tender texture with a hint of sweetness. Diver scallops are more ecologically friendly because they're handpicked by divers instead of being harvested by heavy chain sweeps that are dragged across the sea floor, destroying everything in their path.

**Lobster** One of the most sought-after delicacies from the ocean, lobster has a rich, sweet flavor. There are two different lobster types to choose from, depending on where you live: clawed lobster from New England and the spiny lobster from the Caribbean or California. Lobster is best eaten fresh, and it is normally purchased live. Try to avoid previously frozen.

**Salmon** Eating salmon is healthy because it is high in protein, omega-3 fatty acids, and vitamin D. Salmon flesh is generally orange to red in color. Try to buy wild salmon, when available. If you buy farmed salmon, buy closed farmed fish, which means the fish is separated from the external environment. Salmon should be cooked to medium-rare.

**Shrimp** This is the most popular seafood sold in the United States, so you need to know what to look for when shopping. Wild shrimp have a firm flesh with a sweet, succulent flavor. Farmed shrimp are often tasteless and bland. Select wild-caught shrimp, either fresh or frozen. Avoid imported shrimp, whether farmed or trawled, because of the negative environmental impact.

**Squid** Better known in the restaurant industry as calamari, squid is tender and pleasantly chewy. Calamari must be cooked quickly at high heat to avoid toughness—about one minute. You can buy cleaned squid by the bodies, the tentacles, or a combination of both. I prefer to use more tentacles than bodies because I like the texture better.

**Yellowfin Tuna** Yellowfin has a mild flavor and a firm texture, which make it useful for numerous applications. Avoid buying what is called "burnt tuna," which does not have the typical deep red pigmentation. Burnt tuna is more likely to dry out because it has more water content and less fat. Make sure you buy troll- or pole-caught tuna; just ask your fishmonger how it was caught.

# SHOPPING FOR HERBS AND SEASONINGS

I love the way you can use fresh herbs to add fragrance and flavor to salad. Some have a pronounced flavor and others have a delicate, soft flavor. Herbs can lend subtlety, harmony, and complexity to any dish. They're also very powerful and can overwhelm many things, depending on the amount, so experiment with them first. Too much of anything is not a good thing. It's all about bringing the salad into skillful balance. You will see that I also add herbs and seasonings to my vinaigrettes and herb-infused oils. There's no rhyme or reason as to when to use them; it's all up to you and your palate. When shopping for herbs, try to buy organic.

## Herbs for Salads

**Basil** One of my favorite herbs, sweet basil has slight anise and mint aromas finished with a bright sweetness. The other basil I like to use is Thai basil, with its peppery aroma and slightly licorice flavor. And I like to add opal basil for its wonderful purple color.

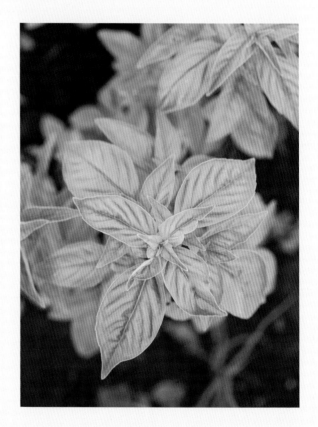

**Chervil** Elegant in taste (mildly licorice) and appearance (feathery, tiny leaves), chervil, a member of the parsley family, is a staple in most French cooking. It combines well with most other herbs, but it has a short life span, so make sure you use it the day you purchase it.

**Chives** The most pleasantly flavored member of the onion family, chives have a great, crunchy texture. I recommend it as one of the herbs to always have on hand at home. It works just about anywhere.

**Cilantro** Most people have a love/hate relationship with this herb. If you can get past the soapy taste of cilantro, you will discover its true refreshing, lemon-ginger flavor.

**Dill** A mild herb with lemon and anise aromas, dill works well with citrus-based salads. A classic pairing is smoked salmon with dill sprigs.

**Fennel** This herb has a straightforward anise taste with a hint of sweetness. It's a great way to add fresh flavor to a salad. You can use the shaved bulb or the delicate fronds.

**Flat-Leaf Parsley** With a clean, mild, and fresh taste, parsley works well with most other herbs. Flat leaf has the best flavor for cooking.

**Lemongrass** I like to use the wonderful citrus flavor of lemongrass when making Asian-inspired dressings. Be sure to pound the lemongrass first, which breaks the fibers to extract the oils, and use only the stalk.

**Mint** Spearmint has a menthol aroma with sweet, tangy, and spicy flavors. I like to pair a chiffonade of basil and mint with fresh melons and berries in the summer.

**Oregano** This well-known herb has a slight bitterness with spicy and peppery notes. I prefer to use this herb in vinaigrettes and infused oils due to its strong flavor. Use very small amounts to accent other herbs.

**Rosemary** A hearty herb, rosemary is like biting into a pine tree with all its pine aromas. It definitely has a pungent flavor, too, so use it sparingly. It makes a great marinade for meats—just add garlic and extra virgin olive oil.

**Tarragon** Hints of pine, licorice, and anise give tarragon a strong flavor, so use it sparingly. It works well with poultry and seafood.

**Thyme** This small evergreen shrub has aromatic notes of earth with hints of mint and clove. I also like lemon thyme with citrus notes. I often use thyme blended in a vinaigrette.

## Salt and Pepper

**Kosher Salt** The main difference between salts is the texture. Cooks prefer to use kosher salt when cooking due to its large surface area. Its coarse, flaky texture is easier to control, and it adheres better when seasoning foods. The size and shape also allow it to absorb more moisture than other forms of salt. Kosher salt contains no preservatives and can be derived from either seawater or underground sources. Due to its fine grain, table salt contains far more sodium that kosher or sea salt; for example, a single teaspoon of table salt contains more sodium than a tablespoon of kosher or sea salt. I prefer to use Diamond Crystal brand kosher salt, found at most grocery stores.

**Sea Salt** The broad term sea salt refers to unrefined salt derived directly from a living ocean or sea. It's harvested from evaporated sea or ocean water and receives little or no processing, leaving its mineral content intact. It has a bright, pure, clean flavor. I like to use *fleur de sel*, an artisanal salt from the Guérande region of France, as a finishing salt sprinkle on vegetables and meats.

**Black Pepper** Black pepper comes from the berries of the pepper plant. Freshly ground black pepper has fruity, woody, and citrus notes. Be sure to use freshly ground pepper through a mill. Preground pepper is dried out and has lost its flavorful oils to evaporation. Black, green, and white peppercorns are actually all from the same fruit. The difference in their colors is due to the varying stages of development and processing methods. Freshly ground black pepper on a salad is almost a must, but how much is personal preference.

## SHOPPING FOR OILS AND VINEGARS

I love to experiment with making dressings. My cooks think I'm a mad scientist when I start creating new dressings for the menu at Mixt Greens. They see me pull everything out of the pantry and throw it all into the Vita-Prep.

By giving you all the tools you need to make a fresh and fantastic dressing, I'd like to inspire you to move away from buying bottled vinaigrettes and dressings at the market for good. With just a few minutes of effort—wow, what a difference a fresh dressing will make! The dressings at the stores are usually loaded with all kinds of crap that you do not need to put into your body. Just pull one off the shelf and start reading the back.

### Making Your Own Vinaigrette

The standard vinaigrette recipe is three parts oil to one part vinegar, which I find way too oily. I mean, I love the taste of a good olive oil, but I prefer not to have glossy lips after each bite. A good rule to use is this: the stronger the acid, the more oil you will need to use to balance the flavors. It all depends on what flavor profile you're trying to create. Sometimes I want the oil to come through as the predominant taste; other times, I prefer the acid. Sometimes I want the prefect balance.

You only need a few tools to make a dressing. A Vita-Prep is my favorite blender for a few reasons: 1) It will emulsify the dressing without emulsifiers. 2) You can throw in whole ingredients, such as shallots, garlic, chiles, and herbs, and the Vita-Prep grinds them all up. 3) There are lots of different speed settings. However, you can also just use a blender, making use of the lowest settings. Of course, there's also the old whisk and stainless steel bowl. I still make a lot of simple vinaigrettes and dressings that way.

Making dressing is basically a two-step process. First, place the vinegar and dry ingredients together and give them a whisk or a quick blend. Second, slowly add a small stream of oil while whisking or blending. If you add the oil too fast, it will not emulsify. If you let your vinaigrette stand for awhile, it most likely will break or separate anyway, but you can prevent this from happening by adding mustard or egg, either of which will help stabilize the emulsion.

Once you start to make dressing at home, and see how easy it really is, you'll never go back to store-bought. You'll discover all the wonderful oils and vinegars that are available and take them home to experiment, just like I do. Currently, the vinegars I like the best are produced from grapes, including Cabernet, Moscatel, Cava, and aged sherry. I am a vinegar aficionado. My pantry at home is full of vinegars from all over the world. Every time I see one, I buy it and try new things with it.

So, explore and remember that a vinaigrette is what ties together everything in a salad, giving you fireworks on the plate and the palate.

## Oils

**Argan** This oil comes from ancient argan trees, a species indigenous to North Africa. It has a very rich, nutty flavor, and, similar to pumpkin seed oil, is a great topping oil. At about $40 for 250 ml, it's very expensive, so use it sparingly.

**Canola** A versatile oil, canola can be used for just about everything. It's never overpowering, and has a light, neutral taste that will complement other ingredients. It also contains less than half the amount of the saturated fat found in olive oil.

**Extra Virgin Olive** Also nicknamed EVOO, extra virgin olive oil is the first pressing of the olives without any refinement. The flavor and style vary by producer—some are buttery, some mild or peppery. The largest producers of olive oils are Spain, Italy, and Greece. I like to use Italian oil from Tuscany as a finishing oil or in a vinaigrette. Do not be cheap when buying it. Trust me, it's worth every penny. On the other hand, always keep cheaper oil in the pantry to cook with.

**Grapeseed** This is one of my favorite oils to use for vinaigrettes. It has a very neutral flavor that complements, rather than overpowers, other ingredients.

**Sesame** Toasted sesame oil has a very predominant flavor and a deep, rich amber color. You only need to use a small amount, because too much can be overpowering. When used in the proper amount, it will add a rich, nutty flavor to your dressing. It's best used in Asian-inspired dressings.

**Truffle** Store-bought truffle oil has an aroma similar to actual truffles but tastes nothing like them. That's what happens when things are made in a lab. Therefore, I make my own truffle oil with chopped summer truffles from Italy and extra virgin olive oil.

**Walnut** The wonderful, roasted nut flavor of walnut oil gives a dressing richness. Extra virgin olive oil and walnut oil work well together. Do not heat this oil, because the delicate flavor will be destroyed.

# Vinegars

**Balsamic** There are two types of balsamic vinegar on the market, the large bottle for $10 or the baby bottle for $50. True balsamic is made from the Trebbiano grape. It has a rich flavor with a nice balance between sweet and sour, and is used to finish dishes. Grocery store or factory-made balsamic is great to use for dressings and marinades. Golden balsamic has no added molasses, leaving its color lighter than common balsamic.

**Champagne** A light and crisp vinegar that has a hint of vanilla, this is a must for your pantry.

**Cider** This vinegar is made from apples. It has a strong acidity level, so make sure you add either honey or sugar to cut the burn.

**Fruit Based** There are many different types of fruit-based vinegars on the market, including raspberry, pear, fig, strawberry, black currant, and cherry. The wonderful sweetness that comes from the fruit complements the acid in the vinegar to give a nice balance. These vinegars are made by adding fruit to either a white or a dark vinegar. Use them when adding fruit to a salad or if you're looking to add a hint of fruit to a dressing.

**Rice Wine** Made from fermented rice, rice wine vinegar has a mild sweetness. It works nicely with citrus-based dressings.

**Sherry** Made from Oloroso sherry from Spain, sherry vinegar has a strong, complex flavor of raisin and nut. This is my favorite vinegar to use in the kitchen. If you feel like splurging, try my favorite: Aged Spanish sherry vinegar.

**Wine Based** I love to use wine-based vinegars, made from either white or red grapes, to make dressings. My favorite specialty wine vinegars include Chardonnay, Banyuls, Cabernet, Moscatel, and Cava. They all have complex flavors and are great for making a simple oil-and-vinegar dressing. It's all you need; just add good olive oil from Tuscany and freshly ground black pepper and salt, and you're off to the races.

## SALAD TOOL ESSENTIALS

Topping my list of tools is a $5 or $10 kitchen scale. I use ounces in some of my recipe instructions because the simple truth is if you try to use cups with something like greens it's never going to be accurate. People might pack in too much or if it's something diced the size of the dice is going to vary greatly between different people. So this is my way of ensuring you're getting precisely the intended balance of flavors in every salad—and you'll find it's much more accurate way of passing your own recipes on to your family and friends, as well.

Here's a rundown of some of the most useful, basic tools out there for making salad:

Stainless steel bowl
Tongs
Salad spinner
Japanese knife
Mandolin
Pepper mill
Measuring cups
Tablespoons and teaspoons
WhiskStick or immersion blender
Vita-Prep or countertop blender

# SPRING

**Park Ave.**
Grilled chicken with asparagus
and rocket

**Gems**
Little gems and apricots with blue cheese

**May**
Fava beans with grilled fennel

**Berry**
Blackberries and strawberries
with goat cheese

**No-Frills**
Mixed spring greens with shaved fennel
and green olives

**Mr. Bean**
Spring lamb with grilled baby artichokes

**Tokyo**
American Kobe beef carpaccio
with frizzled leeks and rocket

**Pentwater**
Grilled asparagus and six-minute egg

**Field**
Butter lettuce and fresh herbs
with Maytag blue cheese

**Sweet**
Haricot verts with sweetbread croutons

**Spring**
English peas with morels

# PARK AVE.
## GRILLED CHICKEN WITH ASPARAGUS AND ROCKET

**VINAIGRETTE**

1/4 cup champagne vinegar

2 teaspoons minced shallot

2 teaspoons Dijon mustard

1/2 cup canola oil

1/2 cup extra virgin olive oil

Salt and freshly ground
black pepper


1/2 pound French fingerling
potatoes, sliced

2 tablespoons extra virgin
olive oil

1 tablespoon chopped fresh
flat-leaf parsley

1 teaspoon chopped fresh
rosemary

Salt and freshly ground
black pepper

1 1/2 pounds boneless, skinless
chicken breasts

1 bunch asparagus

1/2 pound wild rocket

1/4 pound mâche

24 cherry tomatoes, quartered

4 tablespoons toasted pine nuts
(see page 88)

1 cup shaved Parmesan cheese

With the Park Ave., I set out to make a chichi, ladies-who-lunch kind of a salad; basically, a really fancy salad. Grilled chicken with roasted fingerling potatoes, Parmesan, tender asparagus, and a champagne vinaigrette seemed to fit the bill. It's light but luxe. I wanted it to complement a salad I make called the Bachelor, but thought guys wouldn't order it if I called it the Bachelorette. So instead I referenced New York's Park Avenue (but don't tell the guys—they buy it like crazy).

---

Preheat the oven to 375°F and set the grill to medium-high heat.

To make the vinaigrette, combine the vinegar, shallot, and mustard in a blender. Slowly add the oils in a stream and blend until emulsified. Season with salt and pepper and set aside.

On a baking sheet, toss together the potatoes, 1 tablespoon of the olive oil, the parsley, rosemary, and salt and pepper to taste. Roast the potatoes in the oven for 20 minutes.

Season the chicken with salt and pepper and grill for about 15 minutes total, or until cooked through. Let rest for 5 minutes.

Coat the asparagus with the remaining 1 tablespoon olive oil and season with salt and pepper. Grill for about 4 minutes, or until lightly charred, then slice the asparagus into 1 1/2-inch pieces.

In each of 4 serving bowls, toss together 2 ounces rocket, 1 ounce mâche, 6 cherry tomatoes, one-fourth of the sliced asparagus, 1 tablespoon pine nuts, and 1/4 cup Parmesan with 4 teaspoons of the vinaigrette. Season with salt and pepper. Slice the chicken breasts and divide evenly among the bowls.

# GEMS / SERVES 4
## LITTLE GEMS AND APRICOTS WITH BLUE CHEESE

**DRESSING**

$1/2$ cup golden balsamic vinegar

1 teaspoon Dijon mustard

1 teaspoon agave nectar

1 cup extra virgin olive oil

8 little gems

Salt and freshly ground
    black pepper

6 tablespoons Maytag blue
    cheese

4 apricots, sliced

These hoity-toity specialty ingredients should please every blue blood at your table. And get ready for explosions of good taste, because little gems are picked at the most flavorful point in their growth. Maytag blue cheese is one of the most prestigious farm cheeses in the United States.

To make the dressing, combine the vinegar, mustard, and agave nectar in a blender. Add the oil slowly in a stream and blend until emulsified. Set aside.

Peel off the outer layers of the little gems, then slice them in half.

To plate each serving, toss 4 of the gem halves in 2 tablespoons of the dressing and season with salt and pepper. Garnish with $1^{1}/_{2}$ tablespoons blue cheese and 1 sliced apricot.

# MAY / SERVES 4
## FAVA BEANS WITH GRILLED FENNEL

1 pound fresh fava beans

2 fennel bulbs

4 teaspoons extra virgin olive oil, plus more for coating

Sea salt and freshly ground black pepper

Four 1/4-inch-thick slices pancetta, cut into lardons (1/2-inch chunks)

Juice of 1 lemon

1 bunch opal basil

1/4 pound mâche

For this composed salad, I sought an earthy combination, something simple, light, and quick to put together. Fava beans are very mellow and I wanted to enhance the flavor of fennel, so I added basil, for its complementary hint of anise flavor. Throwing it on the grill gives it little bit of a charred flavor and really brings the whole thing together. In addition, the fava beans are soft and the grilled fennel has a snap to it, so you have a great balance of textures.

---

Bring a pot of salted water to a boil on the stove and set the grill to medium heat. Prepare a large bowl of ice water.

When the water comes to a boil, blanch the fava beans for 30 seconds, and then immediately shock in the ice bath. After the favas have cooled, split the pods open with your fingers and remove the beans. Set aside.

Return the water to a boil, blanch the fennel bulbs for 5 minutes, and then shock in the ice water. After the fennel has cooled, slice the bulbs into 1/2-inch pieces, coat them with extra virgin olive oil, and season with salt and pepper. Grill the fennel for about 5 minutes total, or until nicely charred.

While the fennel is cooking, in a sauté pan over medium-high heat, cook the pancetta until super crispy, about 5 minutes, and set aside.

Place 4 pieces of fennel on each of 4 salad plates. Top each with 1/2 cup fava beans and 1 tablespoon pancetta. Drizzle 1 teaspoon olive oil and 1/2 teaspoon lemon juice over all, then arrange 8 basil leaves and 5 sprigs of mâche around the beans. Season with sea salt and pepper and serve.

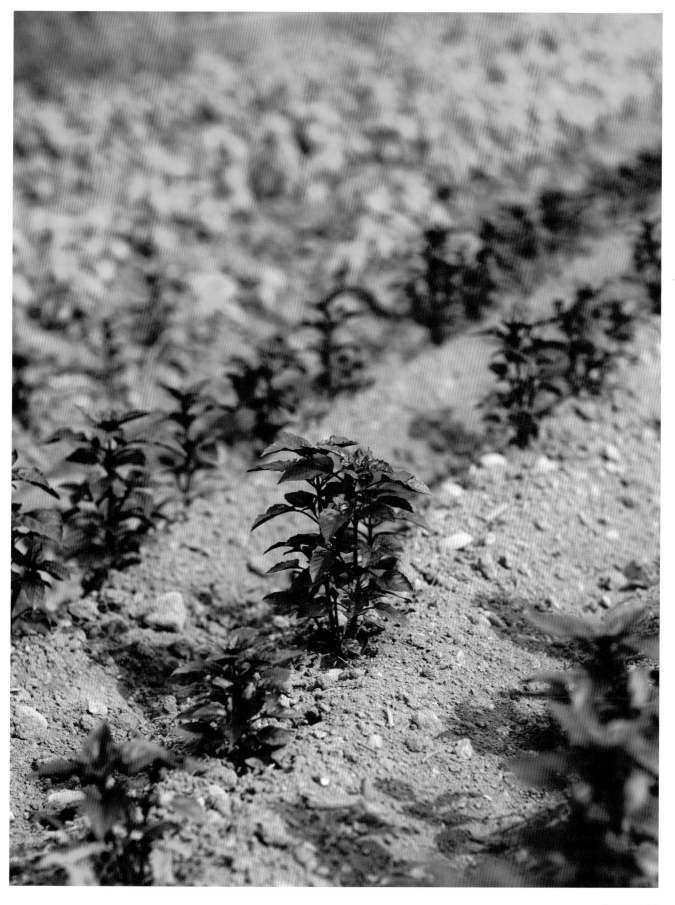

# BERRY / SERVES 4
## BLACKBERRIES AND STRAWBERRIES WITH GOAT CHEESE

### CANDIED PECANS

2 cups pecans

2 tablespoons sugar

2 tablespoons salt

1 teaspoon ground cumin

1 teaspoon ground cayenne

### DRESSING

1/2 cup balsamic vinegar

1 tablespoon minced shallot

1 tablespoon Dijon mustard

1 teaspoon minced fresh thyme
  leaves

1 teaspoon honey

1 cup canola oil

Salt and freshly ground
  black pepper

8 ounces mixed greens

1 pint blackberries

1 pint strawberries, sliced

2 teaspoons chiffonade of mint

2 teaspoons chiffonade of basil

4 tablespoons goat cheese

Salt and freshly ground
  black pepper

A good balsamic and ripe berries taste really, really good together. This salad is a wonderful marriage of the sweetness of strawberries and blackberries, the syrupy tartness of balsamic, the creaminess of goat cheese, and the texture of pecans. All conspire to make a crunchy, fresh, and simple spring salad.

---

Preheat the oven to 350°F.

In a bowl, toss together the pecans, sugar, salt, cumin, cayenne, and 1 tablespoon water. Spread this mixture on a sheet tray and bake for 20 minutes.

To make the dressing, combine the vinegar, shallot, mustard, thyme, and honey in a blender. Slowly add the oil in a stream and blend until emulsified. Season with salt and pepper.

To plate each serving, gently toss together 2 ounces mixed greens, 2 ounces each blackberries and strawberries, 1/2 teaspoon mint, 1/2 teaspoon basil, 1 tablespoon goat cheese, and 1 ounce of the candied pecans with 2 tablespoons of the dressing. Season with salt and pepper.

# NO-FRILLS / SERVES 4
## MIXED SPRING GREENS WITH SHAVED FENNEL AND GREEN OLIVES

1 fennel bulb

$1/2$ pound mixed spring greens

$1/4$ cup chervil leaves

$1/2$ cup green olives, pitted and
   sliced

3 tablespoons fresh
   lemon juice

6 tablespoons extra virgin
   olive oil

Sea salt and freshly ground
   black pepper

Fresh-picked spring greens with shaved fennel, finished
with a nice Tuscan olive oil and sea salt, makes for simple
refreshment and embodies the grassy, clean aromas of
the season.

---

Cut the top and bottom off the fennel bulb. With a mandoline
or a sharp knife, slice the fennel into paper-thin slices.

Place the greens, chervil, olives, and fennel in a bowl and
toss with the lemon juice and olive oil. Season with salt and
pepper and serve.

# MR. BEAN
## SPRING LAMB WITH GRILLED BABY ARTICHOKES

### BEANS

1 pound dried flageolet beans

$1/2$ lemon

$1/2$ cup chopped fresh garlic

10 sprigs thyme

2 teaspoons kosher salt

### LAMB

$1/4$ cup extra virgin olive oil

2 sprigs rosemary, chopped

2 tablespoons chopped
   fresh garlic

8 spring lamb tenderloins

### TAPENADE

$1/2$ cup extra virgin olive oil

1 tablespoon chopped spring
   garlic

$1/4$ cup pitted and chopped
   kalamata olives

Salt and freshly ground
   black pepper

### SALAD

1 red bell pepper

8 baby artichokes

Extra virgin olive oil

2 ounces frisée

Salt and freshly ground
   black pepper

The delicate flavor of spring lamb pairs perfectly with lightly earthy, spring Mediterranean vegetables. I added flageolet beans to round off the salad with a little nutty flavor. As it can be a challenge to find spring lamb, get on over to your best butcher for his help with sourcing.

---

To make the beans, soak the dried beans in water to cover for 4 hours. Drain.

In a large saucepan, combine 8 cups water with the beans, the lemon half, garlic, thyme, and salt. Bring to a simmer and cook for 45 to 50 minutes, or until al dente.

To prepare the lamb, combine the olive oil, rosemary, and garlic in a shallow dish; add the lamb tenderloins, and marinate for 3 to 6 hours, depending on how much time you have and how much flavor you want the meat to absorb.

To make the tapenade, combine the olive oil, spring garlic, and olives in a small bowl. Season with salt and pepper and set aside.

To make the salad, over an open flame, roast the bell pepper until all sides are properly charred, but not completely burnt. Place the pepper in a bowl and cover with plastic wrap for 5 minutes. (This will steam the pepper, making it easier to remove the skin.) Remove the skin and seeds from the pepper, then julienne and set aside.

Bring a pot of salted water to a boil on the stove. Peel off the outer artichoke leaves until you reach a layer where they are almost yellow. Blanch the artichokes for 7 minutes, then let them cool down a bit before cutting each one in half. Coat them with extra virgin olive oil and season with salt and pepper.

continued

Preheat the grill to medium-high. Remove the lamb from the marinade, removing any pieces of garlic or rosemary because they will burn on the grill. Season the lamb with salt and pepper. Grill the lamb for 4 to 5 minutes, or until medium-rare, turning them a few times. Grill the artichokes at the same time, turning them a few times, until you get grill marks on all sides, about 3 minutes. Let the lamb rest for 2 to 3 minutes, then slice.

Place the beans, bell pepper slices, frisée, and artichokes in a bowl with the tapenade. Toss gently and season with salt and pepper. Place the sliced lamb on top and serve.

# TOKYO / SERVES 4
## AMERICAN KOBE BEEF CARPACCIO WITH FRIZZLED LEEKS AND ROCKET

1 pound American Kobe
   beef filet

6 leeks, julienned

1 quart buttermilk

**AIOLI**

1 egg yolk

$^1/_2$ cup canola oil

$^1/_2$ teaspoon fresh lemon juice

$1^1/_2$ teaspoons finely chopped
   kalamata olives

$^1/_2$ tablespoon aged sherry
   vinegar

$^1/_2$ teaspoon minced fresh
   garlic

Salt and freshly ground
   black pepper

4 cups canola oil

2 cups all-purpose flour

3 teaspoons baking powder

1 teaspoon ground cayenne

Salt and freshly ground
   black pepper

2 ounces rocket

4 teaspoons extra virgin
   olive oil

2 teaspoons aged sherry
   vinegar

The Americans are at it again, stealing the prized Japanese Kobe breed (minus the sake massage) and creating wonderful flavors and textures at a tenth of the cost of the foreign products. Yet another reason to go local.

*Note:* Ask your butcher to cut a fresh filet from the center of the tenderloin. Once home, wrap it in plastic wrap and place it in the freezer overnight—this will allow you to slice the filet paper thin.

---

To slice the frozen filet, use a mandoline to achieve the thinnest slices possible. As you are slicing, arrange the slices to cover the bottom of each serving plate, about 8 slices per plate. After all slices are plated, wrap each plate with plastic wrap and place it in the refrigerator.

Place the leeks in a large bowl with the buttermilk. Let soak for 15 minutes.

While the leeks are soaking, make the aioli by placing the egg yolk in a non-stainless steel bowl. While whisking, slowly add the oil in a stream until thickened. Mince the olives, then mix the lemon, vinegar, garlic, and olives into the aioli. Season with salt and pepper and set aside in a small squeeze bottle.

Heat the 4 cups of canola oil to 325°F.

In a large mixing bowl, combine the flour and baking powder. Mix in the cayenne. Working in batches, remove the leeks from the buttermilk and coat them in the flour mixture. Fry them in the hot oil for 1 to 2 minutes, or until golden brown. Remove and season them with salt and pepper while they are still hot. Repeat until all the leeks have been fried.

For each serving, toss together $1^1/_2$ ounces fried leeks and $^1/_2$ ounce rocket with 1 teaspoon olive oil and $^1/_2$ teaspoon sherry vinegar. Season with salt and pepper, then place in the center of the plate over the beef. To finish, drizzle the aioli over the dish in thin ribbons, using the squeeze bottle.

# PENTWATER / SERVES 4
## GRILLED ASPARAGUS AND SIX-MINUTE EGG

**TRUFFLE AIOLI**

1 egg yolk

$1/2$ cup extra virgin olive oil

1 tablespoon aged sherry
vinegar

$1 1/2$ teaspoons chopped fresh
truffle

Salt and freshly ground
black pepper

16 asparagus spears

Eight $1/8$-inch-thick strips
pancetta

Four 1-inch-thick slices
brioche bread

2 tablespoons unsalted butter

1 tablespoon sea salt

4 organic farm eggs

When I think of asparagus, I think of Pentwater, a small
town on the northern peninsula of Michigan where I grew up
eating asparagus in the summertime. Here I'd like to share
one of my childhood memories but with a spin on it: salty
pancetta, rich and creamy truffle, and egg married with the
earthy sweetness of asparagus.

---

To make the aioli, place the egg yolk in a bowl (do not use
stainless steel). While whisking, slowly add the oil in a
stream until thickened. Add the vinegar and truffle. Season
with salt and pepper and set aside.

Preheat the grill to medium. Bring a pot of salted water to
a boil on the stove and prepare a bowl of ice water.

Cut off the bottoms of the asparagus spears. Wrap a strip
of pancetta around the middle of a pair of spears. Grill the
wrapped asparagus bundles for 6 to 8 minutes, until the
pancetta is crispy.

Using a $2 1/2$-inch ring mold, cut out the middle of each
brioche slice. Brush both sides of each slice with butter and
season with the sea salt. Grill the bread, attaining grill marks
on each side.

Cook the eggs for 6 minutes in the boiling water, and then
place them in the ice bath to cool. Peel the eggs and cut them
in half, being very careful not to let the yolks fall out.

Place 2 slices of grilled bread on each of 4 serving plates and
top with some truffle aioli. Place 2 bunches of asparagus on
each piece of bread and top with an egg half.

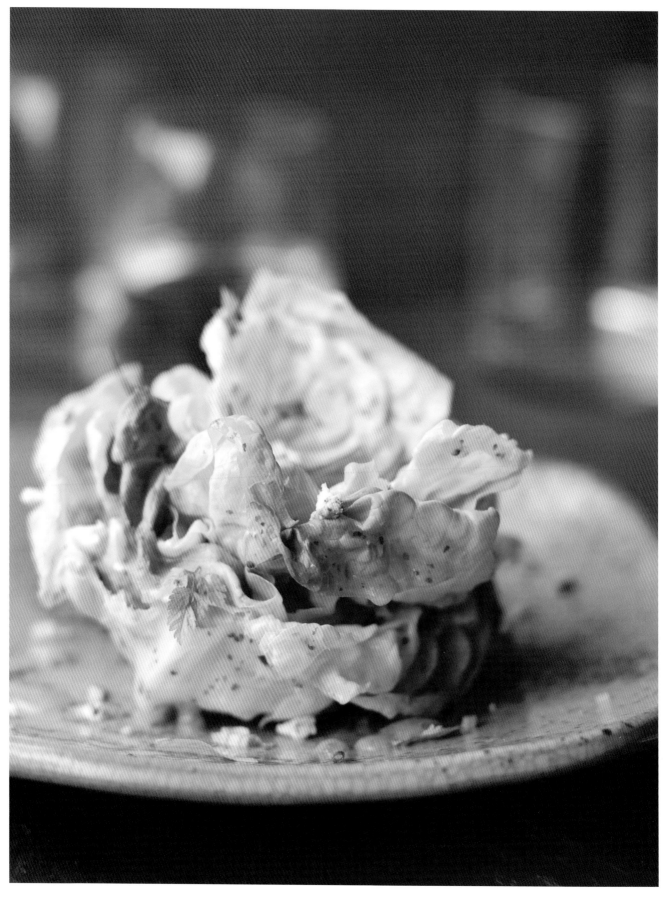

# FIELD
## BUTTER LETTUCE AND FRESH HERBS WITH MAYTAG BLUE CHEESE

**DRESSING**

$1/2$ cup pear vinegar

1 tablespoon minced shallot

1 tablespoon whole-grain
   mustard

$1/2$ cup extra virgin olive oil

$3/4$ cup grapeseed oil

Salt and freshly ground
   black pepper


2 heads butter lettuce

Salt and freshly ground
   black pepper

$1/2$ cup Maytag blue cheese

4 shallots, finely diced

Leaves from 1 bunch tarragon

Leaves from 1 bunch chervil

Hands down every time, Field is what I make if I'm going to
have a salad as a starter. It's creamy and sharp, rich and fresh,
with a little bit of heat from the whole-grain mustard. Classic.

---

To make the dressing, combine the vinegar, shallot, and
mustard in a blender. Add the oils in a stream, and blend until
emulsified. Season with salt and pepper and set aside.

Wash the lettuce and separate the leaves. For each serving,
toss 5 large leaves in 2 tablespoons of the dressing. Season
with salt and pepper. Place the leaves on the plate, stacking
them largest to smallest. Top with 2 tablespoons blue cheese,
1 tablespoon diced shallot, 1 teaspoon tarragon leaves, and
1 teaspoon chervil leaves.

# SWEET / SERVES 4
## HARICOT VERTS WITH SWEETBREAD CROUTONS

1 pound sweetbreads

$1/2$ pound haricot verts

$1/2$ pound cipollini onions

2 tablespoons canola oil

Salt and freshly ground
black pepper

**REDUCTION**

1 cup red wine

1 cup balsamic vinegar

**DRESSING**

5 tablespoons extra virgin
olive oil

2 tablespoons aged sherry
vinegar

$1/2$ teaspoon Dijon mustard

Salt and freshly ground
black pepper

1 tablespoon unsalted butter

Leaves from 4 sprigs thyme

4 ounces frisée

4 strips bacon, cut into lardons
($1/2$-inch chunks) and cooked
until crispy

$1/2$ pound pancetta, cut into
lardons

If you haven't discovered sweetbreads before now, you're in for something special; they're a chef favorite with a texture and flavor that pair perfectly with bacon—hard not to love that. Foodies who already know and love sweetbreads will enjoy the inventiveness of this combination: crunchy sweetbread croutons tossed with a snappy sherry vinaigrette in a bean and cipollini salad with bacon lardons and a balsamic–red wine reduction. Note that this salad needs to be started the day or night before serving.

---

Rinse the sweetbreads, then soak them in water overnight.

The next day, bring a pot of salted water to a boil on the stove. Drain the sweetbreads and cook them in the salted water at a simmer for 2 minutes, then remove and drain. Let them cool for about 1 hour, and then carefully remove the membrane.

Bring another pot of salted water to a boil and prepare a large bowl of ice water. Trim the stem ends of the beans. Blanch the beans in the salted water for about 2 minutes, then remove and shock them in the ice bath. Set aside.

Remove the onion skins and cut each onion into sixths. Heat 1 tablespoon of the canola oil in a sauté pan over medium-high heat. Sauté the onions until caramelized, about 5 minutes. Remove and set aside.

To make the reduction, combine the wine and vinegar in a saucepan over high heat. Cook until the mixture is reduced to $1/4$ cup, about 15 minutes.

*continued*

To make the dressing, whisk together the olive oil, sherry vinegar, and mustard in a bowl. Season with salt and pepper; set aside.

Heat the remaining 1 tablespoon canola oil in a sauté pan over medium-high heat. Break up the sweetbreads into thumb-size pieces, being very careful not to tear the flesh. Season with salt and pepper. Turning continuously to achieve even cooking, sauté the sweetbreads for 4 to 6 minutes, until golden brown. After about 4 minutes, remove the fat from the pan with a paper towel and add the butter and thyme. Baste with the butter for about 1 minute.

In each of 4 individual serving bowls, combine 1 ounce frisée, 1$\frac{1}{2}$ ounces beans, 2 tablespoons bacon, 2 tablespoons pancetta, $\frac{1}{4}$ cup onions, and about 7 sweetbreads. Toss with about 1 tablespoon of the dressing, and then season with salt and pepper. Drizzle the reduction over the salad.

# SPRING / SERVES 4
## ENGLISH PEAS WITH MORELS

2 cups English peas

7 tablespoons extra virgin
    olive oil

2 tablespoons aged sherry
    vinegar

Salt and freshly ground black
    pepper

8 cups fresh morels

2 bunches watercress,
    stemmed

1/4 pound Parmesan cheese,
    shaved, for garnish

One of my favorite times of year is when the first morels come to market. They have a fantastic chewy texture and a clean, yet earthy, nutty flavor. But I'm not alone in my enthusiasm; they're the number one target for wild-mushroom foragers across America.

---

Bring a pot of salted water to a boil on the stove and prepare a large bowl of ice water.

Shell the English peas, then rinse under cold water. Blanch the peas for 2 minutes in the boiling water, then shock them in the ice bath and set aside.

Combine 5 tablespoons of the oil and the vinegar in a bowl, whisking to incorporate, and season with salt and pepper.

Clean and dry the morels. Slice them into little disks. In a sauté pan over medium-high heat, heat the remaining 2 tablespoons oil and sauté the morels for about 4 minutes, or until slightly caramelized. Season with salt and pepper.

For each serving, toss one-fourth of the peas and mushrooms with 1 tablespoon of the dressing. Season with salt and pepper, if needed. Place the mixture on a plate. Next, toss one-fourth of the watercress in 1 teaspoon of the dressing and place on top of the peas and mushrooms. Garnish with the Parmesan.

# SUMMER

## Sour
Grilled sourdough with Brandywine tomato and fresh herbs

## Sol
Summer squash with ricotta

## The Noodle
Soba noodles with enoki mushrooms

## Bachelor
Filet mignon with Roquefort and red leaf

## Cob
Grilled sweet white corn with mixed baby tomatoes

## Maui
Coriander-crusted ahi tuna with mango and avocado

## Pole Bean
Pole beans with warm sherry vinaigrette

## The Greek
Summer tomato and lemon cucumber with fried tulumi

## Picnic
Heirloom tomato with watermelon

## Diver
Roasted corn and hedgehog mushrooms with diver scallops

## Sea
Crab with cantaloupe and caviar

## Fruit Cup
Summer melon with fig and prosciutto

## Leswood
Roasted summer vegetables with portobello mushrooms

## Pure Heirloom
Summer heirlooms with Tuscan olive oil and sea salt

## Steakhouse
Iceberg with all the fixings

## Burger
Ground Kobe with grilled onion

## Summer
Heirloom tomato salad with balsamic vinaigrette

## Fresh
Hamachi with fresh hearts of palm

## Orchard
Grilled summer peaches with Parmesan cheese, rocket, and Treviso

## Spa
Mâche with summer lemon cucumbers and lychee

# SOUR / SERVES 4
## GRILLED SOURDOUGH WITH BRANDYWINE TOMATO AND FRESH HERBS

1 small loaf levain bread

6 tablespoons extra virgin olive oil

Fine sca salt and freshly ground black pepper

2 large Brandywine tomatoes, diced

12 large caperberries, quartered

20 white Spanish anchovy fillets, chopped

1 bunch basil, chiffonaded

1 bunch savory, leaves picked

4 teaspoons red wine vinegar

2 teaspoons fresh lemon juice

Zest of 1 lemon

San Francisco's famous sourdough inspired this version of a panzanella salad. I paired it with some favorite Spanish ingredients like anchovies and caperberries. Their pronounced flavor, along with the savory bread, makes this classic salad my own.

Preheat the grill to medium-high.

Slice the sourdough into 1/2-inch-thick slices. Coat the bread with 2 tablespoons of the olive oil and season with salt and pepper. Grill the bread for about 7 minutes, turning a few times to achieve a nice char and flavor. Let the bread cool, then cut into large cubes.

To plate each serving, toss together one-fourth of the diced tomatoes, 1 cup bread cubes, 3 quartered caper berries, 5 chopped anchovies, 1 tablespoon basil, 1/2 teaspoon savory, 1 tablespoon of the remaining virgin oil, 1 teaspoon red wine vinegar, and 1/2 teaspoon lemon juice. Season with salt and pepper and top with 1/4 teaspoon lemon zest.

# SOL / SERVES 4
## SUMMER SQUASH WITH RICOTTA

4 zucchini

4 yellow squash

4 teaspoons pine nuts

1 pint cherry tomatoes, quartered

$1/2$ cup crumbled ricotta salata

$3/4$ cup extra virgin olive oil

Juice of 1 lemon

1 bunch opal basil, leaves picked

1 bunch mint, chiffonaded

Sea salt and freshly ground black pepper

4 large squash blossoms, julienned

On a hot summer day, this raw salad is the perfect side for a barbecue. The light, fresh, and clean flavors accompany a 2-inch-thick grilled porterhouse to perfection.

---

Using a mandoline, julienne the zucchini and squash. Simply run the vegetable lengthwise down the mandoline, turning after each cut and stopping when you reach the seeds.

In a dry sauté pan over medium heat, toast the pine nuts until golden brown, about 8 minutes. Coarsely chop the toasted nuts.

To plate each serving, toss together $3^{1}/_{2}$ ounces zucchini, $1^{1}/_{2}$ ounces yellow squash, $1^{1}/_{2}$ ounces cherry tomatoes, 2 tablespoons ricotta, 3 tablespoons extra virgin olive oil, 1 teaspoon lemon juice, 10 basil leaves, and 1 teaspoon mint. Season with sea salt and pepper and top with 1 teaspoon chopped pine nuts and 1 squash blossom.

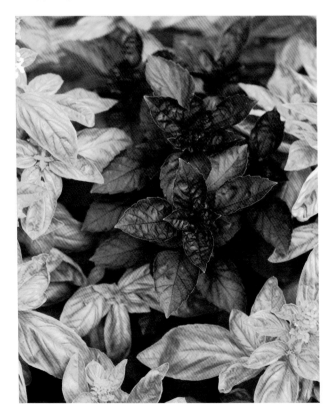

# THE NOODLE / SERVES 4
## SOBA NOODLES WITH ENOKI MUSHROOMS

### DRESSING

1/2 cup rice wine vinegar

1 teaspoon minced fresh garlic

2 teaspoons minced fresh
    ginger

1 tablespoon fresh lemon juice

1 tablespoon sugar

1 tablespoon white miso

1 cup canola oil

Salt and freshly ground
    black pepper


12 ounces soba noodles

1 cucumber

2 (3 1/2-ounce) packs enoki
    mushrooms

4 teaspoons sesame seeds

2 cups pea sprouts

2 red bell peppers, seeded and
    julienned

Salt and freshly ground
    black pepper

Borrowing from traditional Asian flavor combinations, this salad combines toasted sesame seeds, refreshing cucumber, and cool noodles. Miso is a fermented bean paste that I use in the dressing to add richness to this light, healthy salad without adding fat.

---

Bring a pot of salted water to a boil on the stove.

To make the dressing, combine the rice wine vinegar, garlic, ginger, lemon juice, sugar, and white miso in a blender. Slowly add the oil in a stream and blend until emulsified. Season with salt and pepper and set aside.

Boil the soba noodles for 4 minutes, until al dente, then rinse under cold water and set aside.

Peel the cucumber, then slice in half lengthwise and scoop out the seeds by running a spoon down the middle of the cucumber. Slice it into half-moons.

Gently peel the mushrooms apart from each other and set aside. Toast the sesame seeds in a dry sauté pan over medium heat for 6 minutes.

To plate each serving, toss together 1 cup soba noodles, 1/2 cup pea sprouts, 1/2 cup bell peppers, 1/2 pack mushrooms, 1/2 cup cucumber slices, and 2 tablespoons of the dressing. Season with salt and pepper and sprinkle with 1 teaspoon toasted sesame seeds.

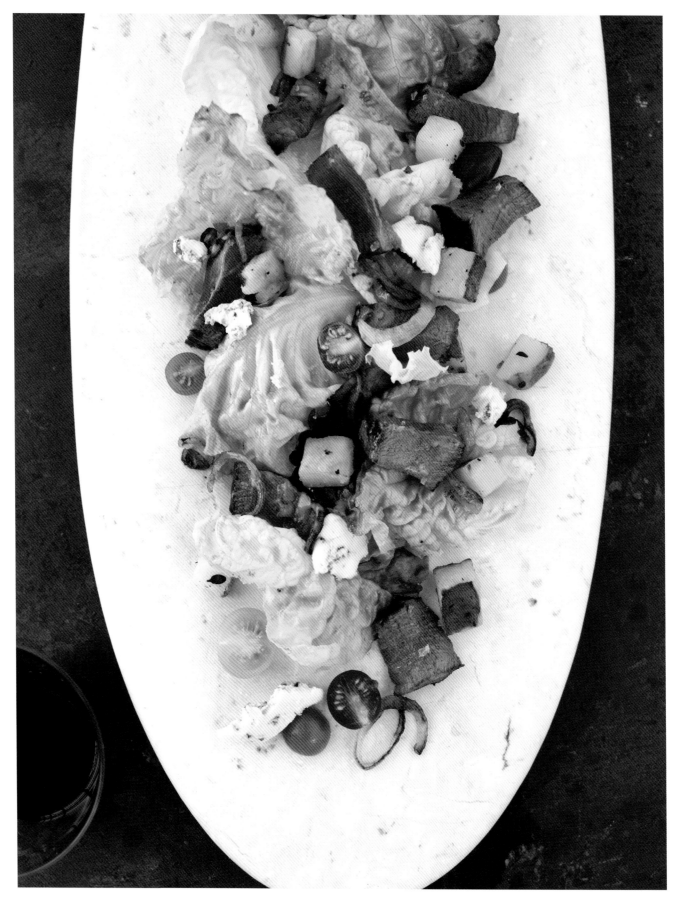

# BACHELOR / SERVES 4
## FILET MIGNON WITH ROQUEFORT AND RED LEAF

2 large Yukon Gold potatoes, diced

1 tablespoon extra virgin olive oil

2 sprigs rosemary

4 sprigs thyme

Sea salt and freshly ground black pepper

### DRESSING

1/2 cup balsamic vinegar

2 teaspoons Dijon mustard

1 teaspoon chopped fresh garlic

1 teaspoon sliced shallot

1 teaspoon honey

1 teaspoon fresh thyme leaves

1 teaspoon sugar

1 cup canola oil

Sea salt and freshly ground black pepper

1 tablespoon canola oil

2 large yellow onions, chopped

4 (6-ounce) prime filets mignons

2 heads red leaf lettuce, leaves separated

2 large Early Girl tomatoes, quartered and sliced

1/2 pound Roquefort blue cheese

You got it, here's what every guy wants to eat all the time: meat and potatoes. I designed this salad at Mixt Greens to win over men and get them to start eating salad. Putting these ingredients together almost forces them to try it— it's one of the bestsellers at the restaurants and has been for more than three years.

Preheat the oven to 375°F. Preheat the grill to high.

In a bowl, toss the potatoes with the extra virgin olive oil, rosemary, thyme, and salt and pepper. Place on a baking sheet and roast for about 20 minutes, or until golden brown.

To make the dressing, combine the vinegar, mustard, garlic, shallot, honey, thyme, and sugar in a blender. Slowly add the canola oil in a stream and blend to emulsify. Season with salt and pepper and set aside.

Heat the 1 tablespoon canola oil in a sauté pan over medium heat. Sauté the onions for 10 to 12 minutes, until the natural sugars caramelize. Season the steaks with salt and pepper. Turn down the grill to medium-high. Grill the steaks for about 7 minutes per side, until medium-rare. Remove the steaks from the grill and let them rest for about 3 minutes before slicing into 1-inch cubes.

To plate each serving (or for all ingredients if serving on a platter, family style), toss 3 ounces red leaf, slices from half a tomato, 2 tablespoons blue cheese, 1/2 cup potatoes, and 3 tablespoons onions with 2 tablespoons of the dressing. Season with salt and pepper and top with the cubes from one steak.

# COB / SERVES 4
## GRILLED SWEET WHITE CORN WITH MIXED BABY TOMATOES

1/2 pint Sun Gold tomatoes

1/2 pint Sugar Plum tomatoes

5 ears fresh corn

1 teaspoon fresh lemon juice

2 tablespoons extra virgin olive oil

20 small basil leaves

1/4 teaspoon kosher salt

Freshly ground black pepper

*Queso fresco*, for garnish

1/8 teaspoon ground cayenne

As the seasons change from spring to summer, the sweet white corn begins to develop in Brentwood, California. In my opinion, it's the best corn on the planet. In Cob, I've take one of my favorite Mexican street foods and put my twist on it by taking it off the cob. The *queso fresco* is a straightforward, slightly salty cheese, and it works with the aromatic basil and the acidic tomatoes. Enjoy this salad on a hot summer day with a 1-inch-thick steak; you choose the cut. I prefer to cook over charcoal to get more flavor—the sweet corn pairs perfectly with the smokiness.

---

Preheat the grill to high.

While the grill is heating up, cut the Sun Gold and Sugar Plum tomatoes into quarters and set aside.

Place the corn, still in their husks, directly on the grill. Grill on high for about 3 minutes, or until all sides are charred. Then turn down the temperature to medium, continue to grill the corn for 15 to 20 minutes, until slightly tender, and set aside to cool.

After the corn has cooled, cut the kernels from the cobs and place in a large bowl with the tomatoes. Toss with the lemon juice, extra virgin olive oil, and basil leaves. Season with salt and pepper. Scoop the salad onto a large platter to serve. To garnish, grate *queso fresco* on top and sprinkle with cayenne.

# MAUI / SERVES 4
## CORIANDER-CRUSTED AHI TUNA WITH MANGO AND AVOCADO

### DRESSING

$1/2$ cup mango purée

$1/4$ cup rice wine vinegar

2 tablespoons fresh orange
  juice

1 teaspoon fresh lime juice

$1/2$ teaspoon chile garlic sauce

2 tablespoons minced fresh
  cilantro

$1/2$ cup canola oil

Salt and freshly ground
  black pepper


1 cucumber

4 (6-ounce) tuna steaks

Salt and freshly ground
  black pepper

4 tablespoons crushed
  coriander seeds

2 tablespoons canola oil

2 heads butter lettuce

1 large Hass avocado, sliced

1 pint cherry tomatoes, sliced

2 ripe mangoes, peeled, seeded,
  and julienned

1 red onion, finely diced

1 bunch basil, leaves picked

$1/2$ cup crushed macadamia
  nuts

The idea behind this salad came from one of my favorite sushi rolls made here in San Francisco: avocado, mango, and macadamia nuts. I added onion, tomatoes, and a citrus vinaigrette to the rich butter lettuce to beautifully bind together all these Pacific Rim flavors.

To make the dressing, combine the mango purée, vinegar, orange juice, lime juice, garlic sauce, and cilantro in a blender. Blend until smooth, then slowly add the oil in a stream and blend again. Season with salt and pepper and set aside.

Peel the cucumber, slice in half lengthwise, then run a spoon down the middle and scoop out the seeds. Slice the cucumber into half-moons.

Season each tuna steak with salt and pepper and 1 tablespoon crushed coriander. Make sure you press the coriander down on the tuna so it sticks. Heat a sauté pan over high heat and add the canola oil. When the oil is about to reach its smoking point, sear the tuna steaks on all sides, about 6 seconds total. After all the tuna has been seared, slice each steak into 3 large pieces and set aside.

To plate each serving, gently toss 4 ounces butter lettuce, 2 ounces avocado, $2^1/2$ ounces cherry tomatoes, $2^1/2$ ounces mango, 2 tablespoons onion, 2 ounces cucumber, and 12 basil leaves with 2 tablespoons of the dressing. Season with salt and pepper. Top with 2 tablespoons crushed macadamia nuts and 1 sliced tuna steak.

# POLE BEAN / SERVES 4
## POLE BEANS WITH WARM SHERRY VINAIGRETTE

1/2 pound Blue Lake beans

1/2 pound wax beans

1/2 pound Romano beans

1/4 cup extra virgin olive oil

1/2 cup finely diced shallots

1/4 cup aged sherry vinegar

1 teaspoon Dijon mustard

2 tablespoons fresh lemon
   juice

Salt and freshly ground
   black pepper

Here I use Romano, Blue Lake, and wax beans, but there's a wonderful variety of pole beans that you can use throughout the summer—so get a variety of what's in season to make this salad. In warm weather, I like the contrast of the cool beans with the warm vinaigrette; it's more refreshing and emphasizes their crisp texture. Try serving this with a simply prepared dayboat halibut.

---

Bring a pot of salted water to a boil on the stove. Prepare a large bowl of ice water.

Cook the Blue Lake, wax, and Romano beans in the boiling water for about 3 minutes, then shock in the ice bath. Let the beans cool, then drain them and place on a serving platter.

In a sauté pan over medium heat, heat 1 tablespoon of the olive oil. Sauté the shallots for about 4 minutes, or until lightly caramelized. Add the vinegar to the pan and deglaze. Add the remaining 3 tablespoons oil, the mustard, and the lemon juice. Whisk together and season with salt and pepper.

Top the beans with 3 tablespoons of the warm sherry vinaigrette and serve.

# THE GREEK / SERVES 4
## SUMMER TOMATO AND LEMON CUCUMBER WITH FRIED TULUMI

2 lemon cucumbers

1 Armenian cucumber

4 ounces tulumi cheese

1/4 cup extra virgin olive oil

1 red onion, finely diced

4 Early Girl tomatoes, diced

1 Marvel Stripe heirloom
tomato, sliced

1 bunch oregano, leaves picked

4 teaspoons red wine vinegar

Juice of 1 lemon

Fine sea salt and freshly
ground black pepper

Playing off a traditional Greek salad, I top this with fried cheese and a nice Spanish vinaigrette. Frying gives firm tulumi a crispy exterior that adds to the salad's texture and further brings out the flavor of the cheese.

Cut the lemon cucumbers into quarters lengthwise, then thinly slice them. Slice the Armenian cucumber a little thicker than the lemon cucumbers into moons.

Slice the tulumi into 1/2-inch-thick pieces, then cut them into long strips. In a sauté pan over medium heat, heat 1 tablespoon of the olive oil. When the oil is nice and hot, place the cheese in the pan and cook for about 1 minute per side, or until golden brown.

To plate each serving, gently toss together half of a lemon cucumber, one-fourth of the Armenian cucumber, 1 tablespoon diced red onion, 1 diced Early Girl, one-fourth of a Marvel Stripe, 10 oregano leaves, 2 teaspoons of the remaining olive oil, 1 teaspoon vinegar, and 1/2 teaspoon lemon juice. Season with salt and pepper. Cut the fried tulumi into medium-size cubes and top each salad with 7 cubes of the cheese.

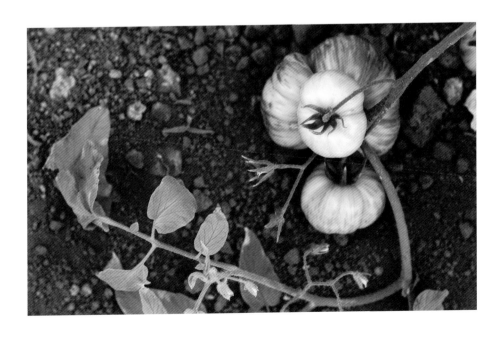

# PICNIC / SERVES 4
## HEIRLOOM TOMATOES WITH WATERMELON

4 pounds seedless watermelon, cut into 1-inch cubes

3 large heirloom tomatoes, cut into 1-inch cubes

6 ounces Greek feta cheese

2 tablespoons extra virgin olive oil

Fine sea salt and freshly ground black pepper

$1/2$ cup fresh basil leaves

$1/4$ cup fresh mint leaves

The Picnic is the most refreshing salad I've ever made. Hands down, if it's hot outside, it's what you want to eat. I'll admit that creating it was a total fluke. People don't think watermelon and tomato go together, but when I tried them I realized that the acid and sweet earthiness in heirloom tomatoes tie into the sweetness and earthiness of the watermelon—and the mint gives it a really great, fresh zing. Use top-of-the-line Italian extra virgin olive oil for the best flavor.

To assemble each salad, place the cubed watermelon and tomatoes in the center of the plate, and crumble $1^1/2$ ounces feta over the top. Drizzle with about $1/2$ tablespoon olive oil. Season with salt and pepper. Top with the basil and mint.

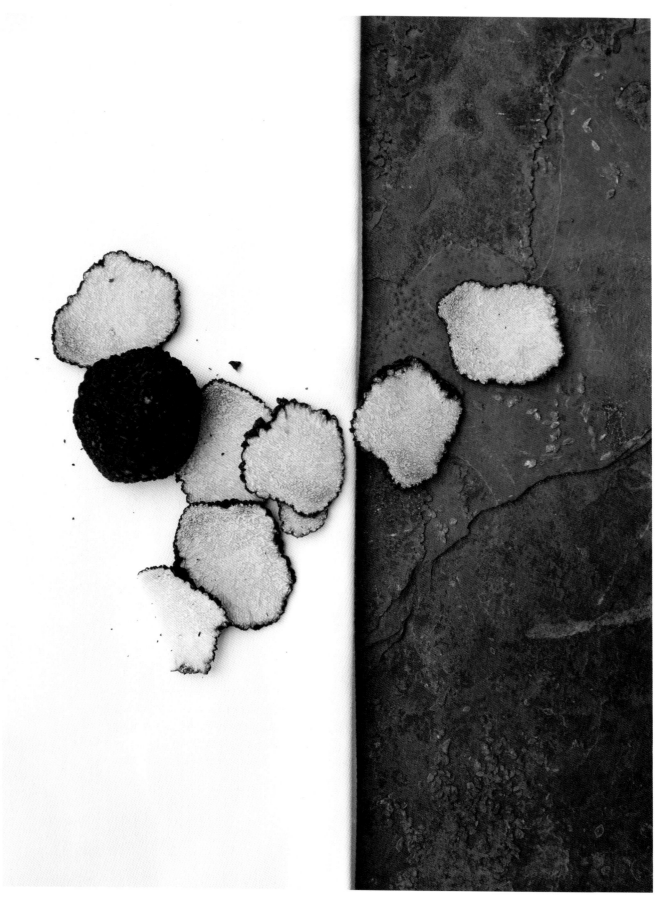

# DIVER / SERVES 4
## ROASTED CORN AND HEDGEHOG MUSHROOMS WITH DIVER SCALLOPS

2 ears sweet corn

**DRESSING**

1 tablespoon chopped shallot

$^1/_2$ teaspoon Dijon mustard

$^1/_4$ cup plus $1^1/_2$ tablespoons
  champagne vinegar

$^1/_2$ cup extra virgin olive oil

$^1/_2$ cup canola oil

Sea salt and freshly ground
  black pepper

$^1/_2$ pound hedgehog
  mushrooms

2 tablespoons extra virgin
  olive oil

1 teaspoon fresh thyme leaves

1 pound diver scallops

Sea salt and freshly ground
  black pepper

1 tablespoon canola oil

4 teaspoons finely chopped
  chives

$^1/_4$ pound rocket

Sea salt

32 shavings summer truffle

A true summer treat, sweet white corn is matched up here with the earthy hedgehog mushroom. And adding the rich, plump diver scallop will make the most finicky foodie's mouth water.

---

Preheat the oven to 375°F.

Place the 2 ears of corn, still in their husks, on a baking sheet. Roast the corn for 15 to 20 minutes, until just tender. After the corn has cooled, shuck the ears and cut the kernels off the cobs.

To make the dressing, combine the shallot, mustard, and vinegar in a blender. While the blender is on low, slowly add the olive and canola oils in a thin stream to emulsify. Season with salt and pepper.

While the corn is roasting, clean and quarter the mushrooms.

Heat the 2 tablespoons of olive oil in a sauté pan over high heat. Sauté the mushrooms for about 5 minutes, until they have released their moisture. Add the thyme and the roasted corn to the pan and cook for about 2 minutes, until the mixture is little bit caramelized.

Trim the foot off the scallops and season with salt and pepper.

Heat the 1 tablespoon canola oil in a sauté pan over high heat. Add the scallops to the pan and sear until golden brown on both sides, about 2 minutes per side.

For each serving, place one-fourth of the corn salad on a plate, then drizzle about 1 tablespoon of the truffle dressing over the top. Add 1 teaspoon chopped chives and a small handful of rocket sprigs. Place the scallops on top and sprinkle a little sea salt on each scallop. Garnish with a few more rocket leaves and 8 truffle shavings.

# SEA / SERVES 4
## CRAB WITH CANTALOUPE AND CAVIAR

**COLVIN VINAIGRETTE**

2 tablespoons champagne
    vinegar

1 teaspoon minced shallot

1 teaspoon Dijon mustard

¼ cup extra virgin olive oil

¼ cup canola oil

Salt and freshly ground
    black pepper


2 pounds fresh crabmeat,
    cooked, shelled, and picked

2 tablespoons mayonnaise

1 bunch chives, chopped

Fine sea salt and freshly
    ground black pepper

1 Tuscan cantaloupe, peeled,
    seeded, and cut into chunks

2 avocados, peeled, seeded, and
    sliced

1 ounce caviar (Sturgeon royal)

I thrive on discovering new flavor combinations, and Sea is a great example of a totally thrown together idea that worked out beautifully. That day I was really in the mood for some crab salad, but I wanted to do something untraditional. One of my purveyors had sent me some Tuscan cantaloupe to try, so I first made a melon emulsion. Then I tossed the crabmeat with my Colvin Vinaigrette (which is basically good on *anything*). I thought that avocado would be great with the melon, so I started with a little melon on the plate, then I layered sliced ripe avocado and the crab mixture with a huge quenelle of caviar I had on hand to top it all off. Honestly, it was like heaven. I had so much crab that I made two mini ones for my two friends downstairs, and they were like, "What the hell is this flavor combination? This is amazing!" Give it a try—it's elegant and just incredibly good.

---

To make the vinaigrette, whisk together the vinegar, shallot, and mustard in a bowl. Slowly pour in the oils, whisking until emulsified. Season with salt and pepper.

Squeeze any excess water out of the crabmeat. Place the crab in a mixing bowl with the mayonnaise, vinaigrette, and chives, and season with salt and pepper. Mix together well and set aside. Purée the cantaloupe in a blender.

For each serving, place 2 tablespoons of the cantaloupe purée in the center of the plate. Place a ring mold on top and fill with a layer of sliced avocado and then crab. Place a dollop of caviar on top of the crab to complete.

# FRUIT CUP / SERVES 4
## SUMMER MELON WITH FIG AND PROSCIUTTO

1 sharlyn melon, peeled, seeded, and cut into medium dice

1 honeydew melon, peeled, seeded, and cut into medium dice

1 cantaloupe, peeled, seeded, and cut into medium dice

$1/2$ pound *prosciutto di Parma*, julienned

1 bunch opal basil, micro leaves picked

4 black figs, trimmed and quartered

$1/4$ pound rocket

$1/4$ cup Tuscan extra virgin olive oil

1 (4 ounce) block ricotta salata, shaved, for garnish

1 tablespoon chile flakes, for garnish

I've been eating fruit for breakfast for what seems like forever, and I'm pretty tired of your average fruit cup. So this salad is a play on a breakfast fruit salad—complete with that breakfast classic pork (parma) and a wonderful kick from chile flakes that'll definitely get you on your toes early in the morning.

---

For each serving, place 2 ounces of each melon in the center of the plate. Place $1/2$ ounce prosciutto on top of the melon, followed by 8 micro basil leaves, 4 fig quarters, and a few rocket leaves. Drizzle about 1 tablespoon olive oil on top and garnish with the shaved ricotta and a pinch of chile flakes.

# LESWOOD / SERVES 4
## ROASTED SUMMER VEGETABLES WITH PORTOBELLO MUSHROOMS

**DRESSING**

1/2 cup aged sherry vinegar

1 tablespoon fresh lemon juice

1 teaspoon minced fresh
flat-leaf parsley

1 teaspoon minced fresh
oregano

1 teaspoon minced fresh thyme

1 tablespoon honey

1 teaspoon sugar

1 cup grapeseed oil

Salt and freshly ground
black pepper

2 sweet rolls, cut into mini
croutons (1/4-inch dice)

2 tablespoons extra virgin olive
oil, plus more for coating

Salt and freshly ground
black pepper

4 portobello mushrooms

1 large sweet onion, sliced

2 zucchini

4 Gypsy peppers

2 tablespoons canola oil

8 ounces mixed greens

4 ounces rocket

1/2 cup goat cheese

Salt and freshly ground
black pepper

I based this recipe on my favorite vegetable sandwich that I cooked while at Gramercy Tavern. If you're a vegetarian, it doesn't get much better than this. At one point this was called Dagwood, but my sister Leslie loves it so much that I named it after her.

---

Preheat the oven to 375°F. Preheat the grill to high.

To make the dressing, combine the vinegar, lemon juice, parsley, oregano, thyme, honey, and sugar in a blender. Slowly add the grapeseed oil in a stream and blend to emulsify; season with salt and pepper.

Place the mini croutons in a mixing bowl and toss with the 2 tablespoons olive oil. Season with salt and pepper. On a baking sheet, bake the croutons in the oven for 10 minutes, or until golden brown, and then set aside. Leave the oven on.

Coat the mushrooms with olive oil and season with salt and pepper. Grill for about 5 minutes on each side, then transfer to the oven and bake for 5 minutes more. Set aside to cool.

Heat the canola oil in a sauté pan over medium heat, add the onion, and sauté for about 12 minutes, or until caramelized.

Cut the zucchini lengthwise into thin slices, coat with olive oil, and season with salt and pepper. Grill the zucchini for 5 minutes on each side, and set aside. Once cooled, cut the zucchini into 1 1/2-inch strips.

Cut the seeds out of the Gypsy peppers, quarter them, then coat with olive oil and season with salt and pepper. Grill the peppers for about 8 to 10 minutes, depending on size, turning to cook all sides. Set aside to cool. After the mushrooms and the peppers have cooled, julienne them.

To plate each serving, gently toss together 2 ounces mixed greens, 1 ounce rocket, 1 1/2 ounces Gypsy pepper, 2 1/2 ounces zucchini, 1 1/2 ounces mushrooms, 1 ounce onion, 2 tablespoons goat cheese, 1/4 cup croutons, and 2 tablespoons of the dressing. Season with salt and pepper.

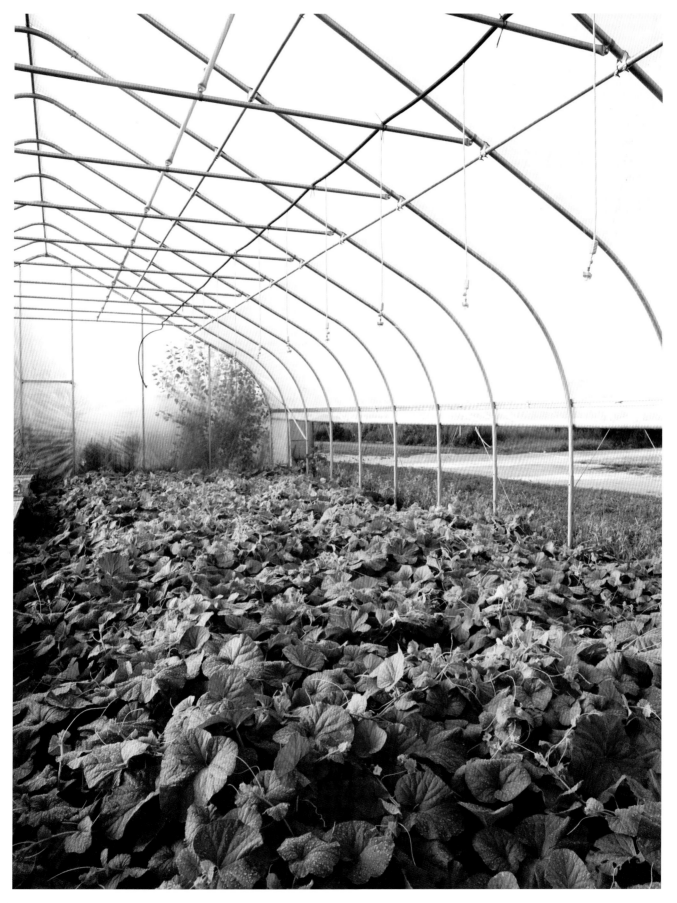

# PURE HEIRLOOM / SERVES 4
## SUMMER HEIRLOOMS WITH TUSCAN OLIVE OIL AND SEA SALT

2 pounds mixed heirloom
tomatoes, sliced into
³/₄-inch-thick rounds

¹/₂ cup Tuscan extra virgin
olive oil

Sea salt and freshly ground
black pepper

¹/₄ cup chiffonaded basil leaves

1 bunch opal basil, leaves
picked

How do you showcase heirloom tomatoes? As simply as
possible. They're one of my favorite fruits, and they don't
need to be messed with. I think all they need is great Tuscan
olive oil and flaky sea salt—and my sea salt of choice is the
Maldon brand from England. Marvel Stripe, Brandywine,
Green Zebra, and Purple Cherokee are all good heirloom
tomato choices for this salad, if you can find them.

---

For each serving, place ¹/₂ pound tomatoes on the plate.
Drizzle 2 tablespoons olive oil on top, then season with sea
salt and black pepper. Top with 1 tablespoon basil and
10 small opal basil leaves.

# STEAKHOUSE / SERVES 4
## ICEBERG WITH ALL THE FIXINGS

1 quart canola oil

**DRESSING**

1/2 cup buttermilk

1/2 cup mayonnaise

2 tablespoons fresh lime juice

4 tablespoons sour cream

1 tablespoon chopped fresh
flat-leaf parsley

1 tablespoon chopped fresh
cilantro

1 tablespoon chopped fresh
chives

1 teaspoon puréed raw garlic

1 1/2 teaspoons chopped
chipotle

1 tablespoon cider vinegar

Salt and freshly ground
black pepper

**ONION RINGS**

1 1/2 cups all-purpose flour

1 1/2 teaspoons baking powder

1 1/2 teaspoons salt

1 teaspoon ground cayenne

12 ounces Negro Modelo beer

3 sweet onions, cut into
1/2-inch-thick slices

Fine sea salt

12 slices smoked bacon,
cut into lardons
(1/2-inch chunks)

1 head iceberg lettuce,
shredded

1/4 pound Point Reyes
blue cheese

1 pint Sun Gold tomatoes,
sliced in half

This is my modern version of a steakhouse wedge, covering all the bases with crunchy onion rings, creamy, sharp blue cheese, a kick of raw garlic, and savory bacon.

---

Warm the canola oil to 350°F in a pot on the stove over medium-high heat.

To make the dressing, combine the buttermilk, mayonnaise, lime juice, sour cream, parsley, cilantro, chives, raw garlic, chipotle, and vinegar in a bowl. Season with salt and pepper and set aside.

To make the onion rings, combine the flour, baking powder, 1 1/2 teaspoons salt, cayenne, and beer in a bowl. Coat the onion slices in the batter and fry them in batches (about 6 to 8 at a time) until golden brown, about 1 1/2 minutes. Set aside on a paper towel and season with sea salt.

In a sauté pan over medium-high heat, cook the bacon lardons until crispy; set aside.

For each serving, toss one-fourth of the shredded lettuce with 2 tablespoons of the dressing in a bowl. Top with 1 ounce blue cheese, 1 ounce lardons, and 1 ounce Sun Golds. Garnish with a stack of 5 or more onion rings, to taste.

# BURGER / SERVES 4
## GROUND KOBE WITH GRILLED ONION

### DRESSING

1 cup mayonnaise

$1/4$ cup ketchup

$1/2$ cup diced kosher dill pickle

2 tablespoons diced shallot

1 teaspoon Worcestershire sauce

$1/4$ cup freshly grated horseradish

1 teaspoon fresh lemon juice

1 teaspoon minced fresh garlic

Salt and freshly ground black pepper

1 large red onion, cut into $1/4$-inch slices

1 tablespoon extra virgin olive oil

Salt and freshly ground black pepper

$1/2$ English cucumber, sliced

$1/4$ cup champagne vinegar

$1 1/2$ pounds ground Kobe beef

12 slices sharp white cheddar

1 head butter lettuce, leaves separated

1 large Brandywine tomato, sliced into half moons

Being passionate about burgers, and not being able to serve them at Mixt Greens, I came up with this idea of a burger salad. Miniature patties are served on butter lettuce with all the accoutrements of a gourmet burger.

---

Preheat the grill to medium-high.

To make the dressing, combine the mayonnaise, ketchup, pickle, shallot, Worcestershire, horseradish, lemon juice, and garlic in a mixing bowl. Season with salt and pepper and set aside.

Coat the onion slices with olive oil, then grill for about 8 minutes total. Season with salt and pepper and set aside.

In a small bowl, combine the cucumber and the champagne vinegar and let soak for 3 minutes.

Form twelve 2-ounce mini burger patties. Season the mini burgers with salt and pepper and grill for about 3 minutes per side. Melt a slice of cheddar on each burger and set aside.

For each serving, place 3 small butter lettuce leaves on the plate, then add a second leaf layer so that each lettuce "cup" is doubled up. Place 1 teaspoon of the dressing in the bottom of each cup. Place a mini burger on top of the dressing in each lettuce cup. Garnish each burger with a slice of grilled onion, a half-moon slice of tomato, and a small slice of cucumber.

# SUMMER / SERVES 4
## HEIRLOOM TOMATO SALAD WITH BALSAMIC VINAIGRETTE

### BALSAMIC ONION VINAIGRETTE

1 teaspoon grapeseed oil

1 yellow onion, chopped

2 cloves garlic, chopped

$1/2$ cup aged balsamic vinegar

1 teaspoon Dijon mustard

Leaves from 4 sprigs thyme

1 cup extra virgin olive oil

1 teaspoon sugar

Fine sea salt and freshly ground black pepper

### SALAD

4 ears sweet white corn

6 large mixed heirloom tomatoes, cores removed, sliced $1/2$ inch think

2 tablespoons extra virgin olive oil

Fine sea salt and freshly ground black pepper

6 ounces Maytag blue cheese, crumbled

$1/2$ cup chopped fresh tarragon

$1/2$ cup chopped fresh chives

$1/2$ cup chopped fresh basil

$1/2$ cup chopped fresh flat-leaf parsley

When summer comes around, the first things on my mind are heirloom tomatoes and corn. Now, most people pair heirloom tomatoes with mozzarella, etc., Caprese style. It's good, but boring. I like to go outside the box, and in searching for a great complement I came up with Maytag blue cheese. It might sound strange at first, but I swear there is something in that pairing that intensifies the flavor of heirlooms—like heirloom tomatoes on steroids. The sweet corn speaks for itself. And word gets around—this salad sells out every day.

---

Preheat the oven to 375°F.

To make the vinaigrette, heat the grapeseed oil in a sauté pan over medium-high heat. Add the onion and garlic and sauté for 5 minutes, until they've caramelized a bit. Add the balsamic vinegar and simmer for 2 minutes, so that the vinegar is absorbed by the onion. Transfer the mixture to a blender. Add the mustard and thyme and blend. While the blender is on low, slowly add the olive oil until the mixture emulsifies. Add the sugar and season with salt and pepper. Set aside.

To make the salad, place the ears of corn, still in their husks, on a baking sheet and roast for 15 to 20 minutes, until just tender. After the corn has cooled, shuck the ears and cut the kernels from the cobs.

Toss the sliced tomatoes in a bowl with the olive oil. Season with salt and pepper. Divide the tomatoes into 4 portions and stack 1 portion in the center of each plate. Top each with one-fourth of the roasted corn, $1 1/2$ ounces blue cheese, and 1 tablespoon of mixed tarragon, chives, basil, and parsley. Drizzle the vinaigrette around the edge of each plate.

# FRESH / SERVES 4
## HAMACHI WITH FRESH HEARTS OF PALM

8 ounces hamachi (sashimi grade)

1/2 pound fresh hearts of palm

**SALSA**

2 tablespoons finely chopped jalapeño pepper

1 tablespoon finely chopped shallot

1 tablespoon finely chopped sea beans

1 tablespoon plus 1 teaspoon extra virgin olive oil

1/2 teaspoon fresh lemon juice

Salt and freshly ground black pepper

1/4 pound sea beans

1/4 cup extra virgin olive oil

4 teaspoons yuzu juice

Sea salt

The distinctive flavor of yuzu adds a wonderful brightness to raw fish. If you've never tried it, grab some at your local Japanese market and experiment. You'll be pleasantly surprised; it's one of my secret weapons for impressing my friends.

*Note:* You'll need to go to a reputable fish supplier for yellowtail or hamachi, and be sure to specify that it's going to be served raw, as sashimi. Ask for about a pound cleaned. You will have a little left over—lucky you. It is not that easy to find fresh hearts of palm, so you might want to do some reconnaissance ahead of time. Sea beans can be found in specialty markets.

---

Slice the hamachi into thin, sushi-sized pieces. You'll need 6 pieces per salad. Put the hamachi on a plate, cover with plastic wrap, and refrigerate while you prepare.

Slice the hearts of palm into about 1/8-inch-thick slices.

To make the salsa, combine all of the ingredients in a bowl and mix, seasoning with the salt and pepper.

For each serving, place 1 1/2 ounces hearts of palm on the plate and season with salt and pepper. Add 5 sea bean sprigs, then drizzle 1 tablespoon olive oil and 1 teaspoon yuzu over the salad. Place 6 pieces of the hamachi on top and sprinkle with sea salt. Finish by garnishing with 1 tablespoon of the salsa.

# ORCHARD
## GRILLED SUMMER PEACHES WITH PARMESAN CHEESE, ROCKET, AND TREVISO

**DRESSING**

$1/4$ cup plus $1^1/_2$ tablespoons
champagne vinegar

1 tablespoon honey

1 teaspoon Dijon mustard

$3/4$ cup extra virgin olive oil

Salt and freshly ground
black pepper

1 white peach

1 yellow peach

$1/2$ pound rocket

1 head Treviso, chiffonaded

1 bunch mint, chiffonaded

1 bunch basil, chiffonaded

1 (4 ounce) block Parmesan
cheese

Salt and freshly ground
black pepper

When peaches are perfectly ripe and juicy at your farmers' market, bring them home and let them speak for themselves with this simple recipe. The spicy and bitter rocket, the ribbons of Treviso, and the aromatic and fresh-tasting basil and mint create a bouquet that's an ultimate palate-pleasing backdrop for the velvety, sweet fruit.

---

To make the dressing, combine the vinegar, honey, and mustard in a blender. Slowly add the oil in a thin stream, and blend to emulsify. Season with salt and pepper.

Slice the peaches so that you have 8 slices per half.

For each serving, gently toss 1 $1/2$ ounces rocket, $1/2$ ounce Treviso, $1/2$ teaspoon mint, 1 teaspoon basil, 4 slices white peach and 4 slices yellow peach with $1^1/_2$ tablespoons of the dressing in a bowl. Season with salt and pepper and shave fresh Parmesan on top.

# SPA / SERVES 4
## MÂCHE WITH SUMMER LEMON CUCUMBERS AND LYCHEE

**DRESSING**

1/4 cup rice wine vinegar

1 tablespoon fresh lemon juice

1/2 teaspoon sugar

1/2 cup extra virgin olive oil

Fine sea salt and freshly
  ground black pepper


1 pint fresh lychees

1 (3 1/2-ounce) pack enoki
  mushrooms

8 ounces mâche

1 pint mixed cherry tomatoes,
  halved

2 lemon cucumbers, sliced into
  half-moons

1 English cucumber

Fine sea salt and freshly
  ground black pepper

This salad reflects the refreshing cucumber and lemon water provided at day spas, post-treatment or workout. The floral fragrance of the lychee is light or powerful depending on how much you use, and the green flavor of the cucumbers seems to pull the impurities right out of you. If you can't find fresh lychees, you can use canned; just make sure to rinse them thoroughly.

---

To make the dressing, whisk together the rice wine vinegar, lemon juice, and sugar in a bowl. Pour the oil in a stream and whisk to emulsify. Season with salt and pepper and set aside.

Peel and chop the lychees. Gently separate the mushrooms from one another.

For each serving, toss 2 ounces mâche, 2 ounces cherry tomatoes, one-fourth of the mushrooms, 2 ounces lemon cucumber, and 1 ounce English cucumber with 1 tablespoon of the dressing in a bowl. Season with sea salt and pepper. Top with 1 teaspoon chopped lychees and a pinch of sea salt. Add more lychees if you would like a stronger floral flavor.

# FALL

### Grove
Honey Crisp apple with Point Reyes
blue cheese

### Heaven
Mixed chicory and chanterelles
with duck egg

### Green
Mixed seasonal apples with Mexican spice

### Porky
Mixed greens with pork tenderloin, roasted
butternut squash, and port reduction

### Grain
Roasted fall root vegetables with farro

### Donald
Duck confit with persimmons
and blue cheeses

### Sprout
Brussels sprouts with warm brown butter
vinaigrette

### Vine
Heirloom grapes with tarragon leaves

### Sonoma
Mixed greens and Cabernet-poached pear
with Humboldt Fog goat cheese

### Autumn
Roasted golden beets with
Cambozola cheese

### Mashup
Broccoli, cauliflower, bacon, and more

# GROVE / SERVES 4
## HONEY CRISP APPLES WITH POINT REYES BLUE CHEESE

**SPICED NUTS**

1 cup walnut halves

2 tablespoons corn syrup

2 teaspoons sugar

$1/4$ teaspoon ground cumin

$1/2$ teaspoon ground cayenne

$1/4$ teaspoon ground coriander

$1/2$ teaspoon chili powder

$1/2$ teaspoon salt

**DRESSING**

$1/4$ cup champagne vinegar

1 teaspoon Dijon mustard

1 teaspoon minced shallot

1 tablespoon honey

1 tablespoon sugar

$1/2$ cup canola oil

$1/2$ cup extra virgin olive oil

Salt and freshly ground
black pepper

1 head butter lettuce

$1/4$ pound Point Reyes blue
cheese, crumbled

2 Honey Crisp apples, cored
and sliced

1 Asian pear, cored and sliced

1 fennel bulb, thinly sliced

Salt and freshly ground
black pepper

$1/2$ cup pomegranate seeds

Leaves from 1 bunch tarragon

When the local apples start being harvested in Sonoma, there's such a wide variety available at the farmers' market that it's hard to pick a favorite, but Honey Crisp is right up there at the top for me. I think their sweetness mixes well with the aromatic licorice flavor of fennel and the finish of a very salty blue cheese.

Preheat the oven to 350°F.

To make the spiced nuts, soak the walnuts in warm water to cover for 3 minutes. In a separate bowl, combine the corn syrup, sugar, cumin, cayenne, coriander, chili powder, and salt. Drain the walnuts, add them to the spice mixture, and toss to coat. Spread the coated nuts on a baking sheet and roast for 20 minutes, then remove from the oven and let cool.

To make the dressing, whisk together the vinegar, mustard, shallot, honey, and sugar in a mixing bowl. Add the canola and olive oils in a thin stream and whisk until emulsified; season with salt and pepper.

To plate each serving, toss 3 ounces butter lettuce leaves, 1 ounce blue cheese, 1 ounce sliced apple, 1 ounce sliced pear, 1 ounce sliced fennel, and $1^1/2$ ounces of the spiced nuts with $1^1/2$ tablespoons of the dressing. Season with salt and pepper and top with 2 tablespoons pomegranate seeds and 1 tablespoon tarragon leaves.

# HEAVEN / SERVES 4
## MIXED CHICORY AND CHANTERELLES WITH DUCK EGG

**DRESSING**

¹/₄ cup aged sherry vinegar

¹/₂ teaspoon Dijon mustard

1 tablespoon minced shallot

1 teaspoon minced
   caperberries

¹/₂ cup extra virgin olive oil

Salt and freshly ground
   black pepper

¹/₂ pound fresh chanterelles

3¹/₂ tablespoons extra virgin
   olive oil

1 clove garlic, minced

Leaves from 1 bunch thyme

1 cup cubed brioche, as mini
   croutons (¹/₄-inch dice)

Salt and freshly ground
   black pepper

4 duck eggs

8 strips bacon, cut into lardons
   (¹/₂-inch chunks)

¹/₂ pound mixed chicory

Of all the wild foraged mushrooms, chanterelles are among the most versatile. They have a delicate, woodsy flavor and a spongy, meaty texture. Their earthy but neutral elegant taste can be paired with most anything. Watch out for the nine-minute egg; it's habit forming.

---

To make the dressing, combine the vinegar, mustard, shallot, and caperberries in a blender and blend until smooth. Slowly add the olive oil in a stream and blend until emulsified. Season with salt and pepper.

Bring a pot of water to a boil on the stove and prepare a bowl of ice water.

Wash the mushrooms gently in cold water, then dry them and pull them apart into quarters. Set aside.

In a sauté pan over medium heat, heat 2 tablespoons of the olive oil. Add the minced garlic and ¹/₂ teaspoon of the fresh thyme leaves, and sauté for 1 minute. Add the brioche cubes and cook until golden brown, about 3 minutes. Season the croutons with salt and pepper while they are still hot, then set aside.

Cook the eggs in the boiling water for 9 minutes, then shock them in the ice bath.

Heat the remaining 1¹/₂ tablespoons olive oil in a sauté pan over medium heat. Sauté the mushrooms for 3 minutes, then add ¹/₄ teaspoon fresh thyme leaves and sauté for about 1 minute longer.

continued

In another sauté pan over medium heat, sauté the bacon lardons until crispy; set aside to drain on a paper towel.

To plate each serving, toss $1/2$ ounce bacon, 1 ounce chicory leaves, and 2 ounces mushrooms with 2 tablespoons of the dressing. Season with salt and pepper. Peel a duck egg and carefully cut it into 4 pieces—it should still be very soft inside. Place the egg pieces on top of the chicory-mushroom mixture, and garnish with 1 tablespoon croutons.

# GREEN / SERVES 4
## MIXED SEASONAL APPLES WITH MEXICAN SPICE

4 Granny Smith apples, diced large

2 Black Jonathan apples, diced large

2 teaspoons fresh lemon juice

**SPICE MIXTURE**

1/4 teaspoon ground cumin

1/4 teaspoon ground cayenne

1/4 teaspoon ancho chile powder

1/4 teaspoon salt

Zest of 1 lime

1 tablespoon chile flakes

I call this my snack salad. Crunchy and light, it's a good one for keeping around when you start getting the munchies.

___

In a mixing bowl, toss together the apples and the lemon juice.

To make the spice mixture, combine the cumin, cayenne, chile powder, and salt in a small bowl.

Transfer the apples to a serving dish and sprinkle the spice mixture over the top. Sprinkle freshly grated lime zest and a few chile flakes over the top.

# PORKY / SERVES 4
## MIXED GREENS WITH PORK TENDERLOIN, ROASTED BUTTERNUT SQUASH, AND PORT REDUCTION

### SPICE RUB

1 tablespoon ground cumin

1 tablespoon ground coriander

1 tablespoon kosher salt

1 tablespoon onion powder

1 tablespoon garlic powder

$^1/_2$ tablespoon mustard seed

1 tablespoon fennel seed

1 teaspoon red chile
    powder

1 teaspoon ground cayenne

1 teaspoon white pepper


2 cups port wine


### DRESSING

$^3/_4$ cup champagne vinegar

1 tablespoon minced shallot

1 tablespoon Dijon mustard

$^1/_2$ cup canola oil

$^1/_2$ cup extra virgin olive oil

Fine sea salt and freshly
    ground black pepper


8 strips apple-smoked bacon,
    cut into lardons ($^1/_2$-inch
    chunks)

1 large butternut squash,
    peeled, seeded, and cut
    into a medium dice

1 tablespoon extra virgin
    olive oil

1 tablespoon chopped fresh
    sage leaves

Salt and freshly ground
    black pepper

This autumnal pork salad highlights the seasonal flavors of apples and roasted butternut squash. Pistachios and spices traditionally go beautifully with pork tenderloin's subtle flavor, and the mustard brings out its depth. The sweet port wine reduction truly ties it all together.

Preheat the oven to 375°F.

To make the spice rub, combine all the spices in a mixing bowl and set aside.

In a sauté pan over medium heat, reduce the port wine to $^1/_4$ cup and set aside.

To make the dressing, combine the vinegar, shallot, and mustard in a blender and blend until smooth. Slowly add both oils in a stream and blend until emulsified. Season with salt and pepper.

In a sauté pan over medium-high heat, sauté the bacon lardons until crispy, then set aside to drain on a paper towel.

In a bowl, toss the butternut squash with the olive oil and sage, and then season with salt and pepper. Spread on a baking sheet and roast for 15 to 20 minutes, or until tender. Keep warm (but not hot) for serving.

*continued*

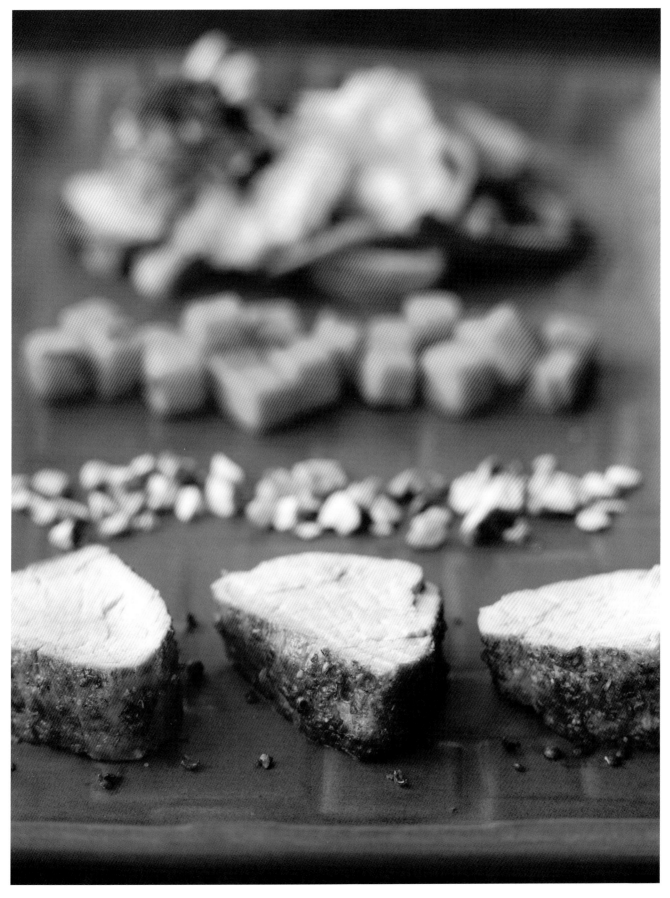

3 pounds pork tenderloin

$3/4$ pound mixed greens

2 Black Jonathan apples, cored and sliced

4 ounces shelled pistachios, chopped

Increase the oven temperature to 395°F. Spread the spice rub on a plate, dredge the pork in the spice rub, coating all sides, and place on a baking sheet. Roast the pork for about 20 minutes, or until the internal temperature registers 150°F on a meat thermometer. Remove from the oven and let rest for 5 minutes. When the pork has cooled, slice into $1/4$-inch-thick slices.

For each serving, toss 3 ounces greens, 2 ounces warm squash, $1 1/2$ ounces bacon, and 2 ounces sliced apple with $1 1/2$ tablespoons of the dressing; season with salt and pepper. Place in the middle of the plate. Top the salad with 4 ounces pork tenderloin. Drizzle 1 tablespoon of the port reduction over the top, sprinkle with 1 ounce chopped pistachios.

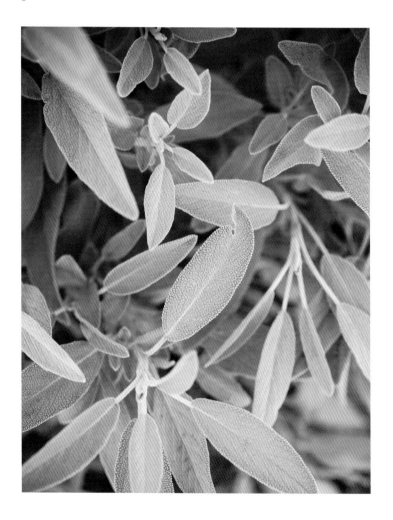

# GRAIN / SERVES 4
## ROASTED FALL ROOT VEGETABLES WITH FARRO

1/2 cup farro

2 teaspoons salt

1 celery root, finely diced

4 parsnips, finely diced

1 rutabaga, finely diced

2 white turnips, finely diced

2 large carrots, finely diced

2 large cipollini onions, finely diced

1/4 cup extra virgin olive oil

Salt and freshly ground black pepper

### DRESSING

1/2 cup red wine vinegar

2 tablespoons lemon juice

2 tablespoons fresh thyme leaves

1/2 teaspoon chopped fresh rosemary

1 teaspoon honey

1 clove garlic, minced

1 cup extra virgin olive oil

Salt and freshly ground black pepper

2 tablespoons finely chopped chives, for garnish

You're about to enjoy the wonderful flavors of roasted root vegetables alongside the hearty texture of farro, guaranteed to keep anyone satisfied on a brisk fall night.

Preheat the oven to 375°F.

In a saucepan over medium heat, combine the farro, 4 cups water, and the salt. Simmer for 30 minutes, or until al dente and a little chewy.

In a mixing bowl, toss the celery root, parsnips, rutabaga, turnips, carrots, and onions with the olive oil. Season with salt and pepper. Spread the vegetables on a baking sheet and roast for about 25 minutes, or until golden brown.

To make the dressing, combine the vinegar, lemon juice, thyme, rosemary, honey, and garlic in a blender and blend until smooth. Slowly add the oil in a stream and blend until emulsified. Season with salt and pepper.

In a large serving bowl, gently toss together the vegetables, farro, and about 2 tablespoons of the dressing. Check for seasoning and serve the salad warm, garnished with the chives.

# DONALD / SERVES 4
## DUCK CONFIT WITH PERSIMMONS AND BLUE CHEESES

**CONFIT**

6 large duck legs

3 tablespoons kosher salt

Freshly ground black pepper

4 cloves garlic, chopped

2 shallots, peeled and chopped

8 sprigs thyme

5 cups duck fat

**VINAIGRETTE**

$1/2$ cup aged sherry vinegar

$1^1/_2$ teaspoons Dijon mustard

1 tablespoon minced shallot

$1^1/_2$ teaspoons honey

$1/2$ cup canola oil

$1/2$ cup extra virgin olive oil

Sea salt and freshly ground
    black pepper

2 Belgian endives, julienned

2 bunches frisée, trimmed

1 head radicchio

Leaves from 1 bunch
    flat-leaf parsley

$1/4$ pound Stilton cheese,
    crumbled

$1/4$ pound Point Reyes cheese,
    crumbled

4 persimmons, sliced paper-
    thin into half-moons

Salt and freshly ground
    black pepper

I love duck confit. I'm a huge fan of the rich flavor and the tender texture, plus it's easy to buy it ready-made these days if you don't have the time to make it. In this salad, I highlight persimmons, which are underutilized and amazing with this game bird. You'll have some extra duck confit to do what you like with—I always like to have extra to snack on. I'm sure it won't stay around for long!

---

Season the duck legs with the salt and pepper. Arrange the garlic, shallots, and thyme on a baking sheet and place the seasoned duck legs on top. Refrigerate, covered, for 24 hours.

Preheat the oven to 225°F.

Remove the duck from the refrigerator and wipe off the salt and pepper. In a large saucepan over medium heat, heat the duck fat until melted. Place the duck legs in a casserole dish and cover with the fat. Bake for 2 to 3 hours, or until the meat falls off the bone. (Note: Never let the fat get too hot; it should just have a few bubbles while cooking.) Remove from the oven and let cool. Remove the legs from the fat, then carefully separate the meat from the bones, ideally keeping the meat in one piece.

To make the vinaigrette, combine the vinegar, mustard, shallot, and honey in a blender and blend until smooth. Slowly add the canola and olive oils in a stream and blend until emulsified. Season with salt and pepper.

Melt 2 tablespoons of the the cooled duck fat in a sauté pan over medium-high heat. Place the duck legs in the pan, skin side down, and sauté until brown and crisp, 2 to 4 minutes. Remove the duck from the pan and cut the meat into long strips. Set aside.

For each serving, toss 1 ounce endive, 1 ounce frisée, a few radicchio leaves, 8 parsley leaves, $1/4$ ounce each Stilton and Point Reyes, and 12 slices persimmon with 5 teaspoons of the dressing. Season with salt and pepper. Place the mixture on the plate and top with 2 ounces duck meat, crispy side up.

FALL **103**

# SPROUT / SERVES 4
## BRUSSELS SPROUTS WITH WARM BROWN BUTTER VINAIGRETTE

2 pounds Brussels sprouts (should yield 12 ounces of leaves)

8 strips bacon, cut into lardons ($1/_2$-inch chunks)

1 tablespoon chopped fresh sage

1 tablespoon Dijon mustard

$1/_4$ cup cider vinegar

$1^1/_2$ tablespoons unsalted butter

1 Fuji apple, cored and sliced $1/_8$ inch thick

Salt and freshly ground black pepper

$1/_2$ cup pomegranate seeds

1 white turnip, julienned

As a child, I used to feed the Brussels sprouts my mom would make for dinner to my dog under the table—and the dog didn't even want to eat them. Over the years, I've grown to appreciate them, however. The leaves taste earthy and delicious, and have a sweet, savory bitterness. I added the turnip to the mix for its raw crunch.

Bring a pot of salted water to a boil on the stove and prepare a large bowl of ice water.

Remove the bottom of each sprout and peel apart all the leaves. Blanch the leaves for 2 minutes in the boiling water, then shock them in the ice bath; drain and set aside.

In a sauté pan over medium-high heat, sauté the bacon until golden brown, about 5 minutes. Transfer the bacon to a plate and set aside. Drain the fat from the pan. Add the butter to the pan and let it slowly melt, browning slightly, then add the sage and sauté for 1 minute to infuse the butter. Add the mustard and vinegar to the pan, then whisk the mixture until emulsified.

Place the sprout leaves in a serving bowl or on a platter and toss with the apple slices. Top with the brown butter vinaigrette. Season with salt and pepper and garnish with the bacon, pomegranate seeds, and turnip.

# VINE
## HEIRLOOM GRAPES WITH TARRAGON LEAVES

**DRESSING**

$1/2$ cup golden balsamic vinegar

1 teaspoon whole-grain
   mustard

1 teaspoon maple syrup

$1/4$ teaspoon ground cinnamon

1 cup grapeseed oil

Salt and freshly ground black
   pepper


1 bunch (6 ounces) red grapes

1 bunch (6 ounces) green grapes

1 bunch (6 ounces) black grapes

1 head fennel, sliced paper-thin

Leaves from 4 bunches
   tarragon

Leaves from 1 bunch opal basil

Salt and freshly ground
   black pepper

$1/4$ pound Manchego cheese,
   for garnish

This salad could be served at any time of the year, but since
I live in northern California I start thinking about grapes
during harvest in the fall. I've made this for my winemaker
friends, who, at the end of a long day of pressing them, know
and love their grapes better than anybody.

---

To make the dressing, whisk together the vinegar, mustard,
maple syrup, and cinnamon in a bowl. Add the grapeseed oil
in a thin stream and whisk until emulsified. Season with salt
and pepper.

Slice all of the grapes in half.

To plate each serving, toss 2 ounces fennel, $1^1/2$ ounces each
type of grape, 2 tablespoons (.02 ounce) tarragon leaves, and
10 basil leaves with $1^1/2$ tablespoons of the dressing. Season
with salt and pepper and shave the Manchego cheese over
the top.

# SONOMA / SERVES 4
## MIXED GREENS AND CABERNET-POACHED PEAR WITH HUMBOLDT FOG GOAT CHEESE

**POACHING LIQUID**

1 (750-ml) bottle Cabernet
 or Zinfandel

1 cup port wine

1 cinnamon stick

1 bay leaf

2 Bartlett pears

1/2 cup coarsely chopped
 pecans

**DRESSING**

1/2 cup cider vinegar

1/2 cup currants

1 cup grapeseed oil

Salt and freshly ground
 black pepper

1/4 pound Humboldt Fog
 goat cheese

1/4 pound rocket

1 head radicchio, leaves
 separated

Salt and freshly ground
 black pepper

Starting a meal with a spicy cabernet-poached pear salad on a chilly fall night is a great way to usher in the season. Humboldt Fog goat cheese is a wonderful local selection where I live; it's chalky on the outside and creamy in the middle. Seek out a similar goat cheese from your area.

---

To make the poaching liquid, combine the red wine, port, 1 cup water, the cinnamon stick, and bay leaf in a pot over medium heat. While the poaching liquid is being brought to a simmer, peel the pears and cut them in half. Poach the pears in the simmering liquid for about 1 hour and 15 minutes, checking them after 45 minutes. Pierce each pear with a knife to test for doneness. You're cooking them at a low temperature to infuse the flavor of the wine and herbs so they should remain somewhat firm; you do not want them to become mushy.

Preheat the oven to 350°F.

Spread the pecans on a baking sheet and roast for 6 minutes. Transfer to a plate to cool.

To make the dressing, combine the vinegar and currants in a blender and blend until smooth. Slowly add the oil in a thin stream and blend until emulsified. Season with salt and pepper.

Slice the goat cheese into thin slices. Be careful not to break the cheese pieces when slicing, because they are very fragile. Remove the pears from the poaching liquid, and core and slice them.

To plate each serving, toss 1 1/2 ounces rocket, 1 ounce radicchio, 1 ounce of the toasted pecans, and 2 1/2 ounces of the poached pears with 4 teaspoons of the dressing; season with salt and pepper. Top the salad with 1 ounce sliced goat cheese.

# WINTER

## Spears
Grilled romaine with Meyer lemon

## Beet-neck
Tangerine and golden beet salad

## Siam
Gulf shrimp with mango and green papaya

## Cabo
Mango and avocado with lime

## Lobster Boat
Poached lobster with roasted golden beets

## Navel
Cara Cara oranges with Marcona
almonds and picholine olives

## Castle
Castelfranco with a six-minute egg
and avocado

## Bunny
Moroccan-style baby carrot salad
with citrus

## San Sebastian
Chorizo and dates with greens

## Monterey
Squid and gigante beans with chorizo

## Phuket
Grilled hanger steak with
buckwheat noodles

## Indo
Grapefruit and jicama with Thai basil

## Passion
Crab and citrus with passion fruit

## Bistro
Filet of beef with proper fixings

## Tropical
Mixed citrus and fresh coconut

## Egghead
Farm egg with caviar and poached
quail egg

## Classic
Heart of romaine with mini croutons

## Captiva
Butter lettuce with citrus and avocado

## Crudo
Arctic char with fresh horseradish

## Tower
Tuna tartare

## Treat
Roasted fingerling potatoes with herbs
and truffle cheese

# SPEARS
## GRILLED ROMAINE WITH MEYER LEMON

4 hearts romaine

$1/4$ cup extra virgin olive oil, plus more for coating

Juice of 2 Meyer lemons

Sea salt and freshly ground black pepper

$1/4$ pound Parmesan cheese

16 Spanish white anchovies

Let's be honest: romaine is boring. I am tired of seeing plain, watery romaine. But by charring the romaine on the grill, I've added a wonderful smokiness and nuttiness to the leaves that enhances their slightly bitter flavor. The aromatic Meyer lemon is a vibrant citrus whose bright acid that pairs perfectly with grilled romaine.

---

Preheat the grill to high.

Cut the hearts of romaine in half and coat in olive oil. Place on the grill and turn to achieve light grill marks on all sides. Remove from the grill. Trim off the bottom of each one, then cut each heart of romaine in half again.

Place the romaine on a large platter. Drizzle with the $1/4$ cup olive oil and the lemon juice and season with sea salt and black pepper. Shave fresh Parmesan on top. Place 1 anchovy on each heart and serve.

# BEET-NECK / SERVES 4
## TANGERINE AND GOLDEN BEET SALAD

1 pound golden baby beets

4 teaspoons pine nuts

Salt and freshly ground black pepper

1 pound Pixie tangerines, peeled and sliced

2 teaspoons fresh Meyer lemon juice

4 teaspoons extra virgin olive oil

2 teaspoons finely diced shallot

2 teaspoons chiffonaded basil (opal basil and regular)

In the wintertime, I look forward to the arrival of bright, fresh citrus because it pairs so well with these sweet, roasted baby beets. It's a simple, elegant flavor combination.

---

Preheat the oven to 350°F.

Roast the baby beets on a baking sheet in the oven for 15 to 20 minutes, or until tender. Toast the pine nuts on another baking sheet for 8 minutes, then remove from the oven. While the beets are still warm, remove their skins by gently rubbing with a towel. After the beets have cooled, slice off the top and bottom of each beet, then cut them in half. Season with salt and pepper.

For each serving, arrange 5 beet pieces and 5 tangerine slices on the plate. Drizzle $1/2$ teaspoon lemon juice and 1 teaspoon olive oil on top. Sprinkle with $1/2$ teaspoon shallot, 1 teaspoon of the toasted pine nuts, and $1/2$ teaspoon basil. Season with salt and pepper.

# SIAM / SERVES 4
## GULF SHRIMP WITH MANGO AND GREEN PAPAYA

**MARINADE**

2 cups fresh orange juice

2 tablespoons chopped
    jalapeño pepper

3 tablespoons chopped fresh
    garlic

3 tablespoons chopped fresh
    ginger

Freshly ground black pepper

20 large fresh Gulf shrimp,
    peeled and deveined

**DRESSING**

1/4 cup fresh lime juice

1 1/2 teaspoons minced Thai
    bird chile

1/4 cup rice wine vinegar

1 teaspoon fish sauce

1/2 teaspoon soy sauce

1 tablespoon minced fresh
    garlic

1 tablespoon minced
    lemongrass

1 teaspoon sugar

1/2 cup canola oil

Salt and freshly ground
    black pepper

1 cup unsalted peanuts

**CHIPOTLE HONEY**

2 teaspoons chopped canned
    chipotle chile

3/4 cup honey

Salt and freshly ground black
    pepper

I made a Thai-influenced salad, then in a last-minute thought, which happens often, I added the chipotle honey, which really brings it together. Its heat and smokiness paired perfectly with the fruit and made the dish.

*Note:* I recommend using a mandoline to julienne the green papaya, because it can be very tough.

---

To make the marinade, combine the orange juice, jalapeño, garlic, ginger, and 1 teaspoon freshly ground black pepper in a bowl. Add the shrimp and let marinate in the refrigerator for 4 hours.

To make the dressing, combine the lime juice, chile, vinegar, fish sauce, soy sauce, garlic, lemongrass, and sugar in a blender. Slowly add the canola oil in a stream, and blend until emulsified. Season with salt and pepper and set aside.

Preheat the oven to 300°F and preheat the grill to high.

Spread the peanuts on a baking sheet and roast in the oven for 15 minutes. Let cool, then chop and set aside.

To make the chipotle honey, add the honey and chipotle chile to a blender and pulse to combine. Set aside.

Remove the shrimp from the marinade, season with salt and pepper, and grill for 4 to 5 minutes, or until opaque, flipping once.

continued

1 daikon radish, diced

2 mangoes, cored, peeled, and julienned

1 green papaya, peeled, seeded, and julienned

1 red bell pepper, finely diced

2 shallots, finely diced

Leaves from 1 bunch cilantro

1 bunch basil, chiffonaded

1 bunch mint, chiffonaded

To plate each serving, combine $1/4$ cup daikon, 1 cup mango, 1 cup papaya, 3 tablespoons bell pepper, 1 tablespoon shallot, 2 tablespoons cilantro leaves, 2 tablespoons basil, and 2 teaspoons mint with $2^1/2$ tablespoons of the dressing. Place 5 shrimp on top, garnish with 2 tablespoons of the roasted peanuts, and drizzle with $1^1/2$ teaspoons of the chipotle honey.

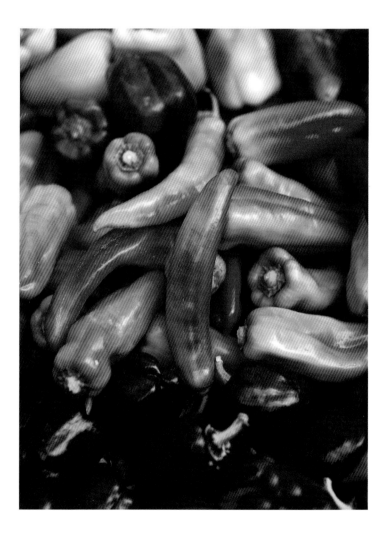

# CABO
## MANGO AND AVOCADO WITH LIME

2 avocados, peeled, seeded, and sliced

2 mangoes, peeled, seeded, and sliced

Juice of 2 limes

1 large jalapeño pepper, diced

1 red onion, diced

Leaves from 1 bunch cilantro

Salt and freshly ground black pepper

This dish was inspired by street food that I've had in Cabo San Lucas, Mexico. I've added some avocado for richness.

---

For each serving, place 5 avocado slices and 6 mango slices on the plate. Drizzle 1 teaspoon fresh lime juice on top. Garnish with 1 teaspoon jalapeño, 1 teaspoon red onion, and 7 cilantro leaves. Season with salt and pepper.

# LOBSTER BOAT / SERVES 4
## POACHED LOBSTER WITH ROASTED GOLDEN BEETS

### ROASTED BEETS

4 golden beets, cut into ³/₄-inch chunks

Extra virgin olive oil, for roasting

Salt and freshly ground black pepper

### VINAIGRETTE

Juice of ¹/₂ Meyer lemon

¹/₄ cup champagne vinegar

1 tablespoon agave nectar

1 cup extra virgin olive oil

Salt and freshly ground black pepper

### PICKLED ONION

1 large red onion, thinly sliced

1 cup cider vinegar

¹/₄ cup fresh lime juice

1 jalapeño pepper, finely diced

1 tablespoon sugar

This is by far my favorite salad in the book. The earthiness of the beets paired with the sweet, rich flavor of the lobster and finished with the spicy pickled onion will make your tastebuds sing.

---

Preheat the oven to 350°F.

To make the roasted beets, lightly coat the beets with olive oil and season with salt and pepper. Roast them on a baking sheet in the oven for about 1 hour, or until fork-tender. Let cool, then use a paper towel to rub off the skins.

While the beets are cooking, make the vinaigrette by placing the lemon juice, vinegar, and agave nectar in a blender. Slowly add the olive oil in a stream, and blend until emulsified. Season with salt and pepper and set aside.

To make the pickled onion, combine the onion, vinegar, lime juice, jalapeño, and sugar in a bowl. Let the mixture marinate for 1 hour.

continued

¹/₄ cup pine nuts

Two 1¹/₂-pound live lobsters

¹/₂ cup unsalted butter

Leaves from 1 bunch tarragon

1 pound mâche

Salt and freshly ground
    black pepper

In a dry sauté pan over medium heat, toast the pine nuts until browned, about 8 minutes. Transfer to a plate to cool.

Bring a large pot of salted water to a boil on the stove and prepare a large bowl of ice water.

The most humane way to kill a lobster at home is to use a very sharp chef's knife to slice the lobster's head in half; use one swift motion. Do this with each lobster, then separate the lobster claws (with knuckles attached) and tails from the bodies.

Place the claws and tails in the boiling water and cover the pot. Cook the lobster tails for 6 minutes, then place in the ice bath. Cook the claws for 8 minutes, then place in the ice bath. After the lobster has cooled, remove the meat from the claws, knuckles, and tails (keeping the meat intact). Cut the lobster into medium-size pieces.

In a saucepan over medium heat, melt the butter. Add the tarragon and stir to combine. Place the lobster meat in the butter and poach for 2 minutes, then set aside.

Toss 4 sprigs of mâche and 5 pieces of beet with the vinaigrette and season with salt and pepper.

For each serving, make a bed of the dressed mâche and beets on the salad plate. Place 6 chunks of the lobster meat and 5 slices of the pickled onion on top, and garnish with 1 teaspoon of the toasted pine nuts.

# NAVEL / SERVES 4
## CARA CARA ORANGES WITH MARCONA ALMONDS AND PICHOLINE OLIVES

1 head Treviso

4 heads Belgian endive

2 Cara Cara oranges

$1/4$ pound Marcona almonds

1 cup picholine olives, pits
removed

$1/4$ pound rocket

$1/4$ cup extra virgin olive oil

4 teaspoons red wine vinegar

Sea salt and freshly ground
black pepper

$1/4$ pound Manchego cheese

I like this salad's play on briny, acidic, and nutty flavors with a hint of bitterness from the Treviso. Try serving it with fish, perhaps day boat halibut, to take full advantage of its clean, bright-on-your-palette notes.

---

Julienne the Treviso and endive and set aside. Peel the oranges, cut them in half, then slice them into half-moon cross-sections. Coarsely chop the almonds and olives.

To plate each serving, toss 1 ounce rocket, $1/2$ ounce Treviso, 1 ounce endive, and $2^1/2$ ounces orange with 2 teaspoons olive oil and 1 teaspoon red wine vinegar. Season with sea salt and black pepper. Top each serving with $1/2$ ounce chopped almonds, 1 teaspoon chopped olives, and some shaved Manchego cheese to taste.

WINTER **125**

# CASTLE / SERVES 4

## CASTELFRANCO WITH A SIX-MINUTE EGG AND AVOCADO

**CROUTONS**

1 sweet roll

2 tablespoons extra virgin
  olive oil

Sea salt and freshly ground
  black pepper

**DRESSING**

1 cup mayonnaise

$1/2$ cup sour cream

$1^1/_2$ tablespoons champagne
  vinegar

2 tablespoons fresh lemon
  juice

2 salt-packed anchovies

1 clove garlic

$1/_4$ cup chopped chives

$1/_4$ cup chopped fresh
  flat-leaf parsley

8 strips bacon, cut into lardons
  ($1/_2$-inch chunks)

1 head Castelfranco

4 organic farm eggs

1 avocado, peeled, pitted,
  quartered, and chopped

Sea salt and freshly ground
  black pepper

In the chicory family, Castelfranco is one of the least bitter. Okay, it's still bitter, but it is more delicate, so go hunt some down. If you've had less than happy moments with bitter chicory, you may be pleasantly surprised; I've created this salad to tempt you to give it a go.

Preheat the oven to 375°F. Bring a pot of salted water to a boil on the stove and prepare a bowl of ice water.

To make the croutons, slice and cube the sweet roll to make 1 cup of mini croutons. Place the bread in a bowl and toss with the olive oil and season with a pinch of salt and pepper. Spread the croutons on a baking sheet and bake for 10 minutes, or until golden brown. Let cool and set aside.

To make the dressing, combine the mayonnaise, sour cream, vinegar, lemon juice, anchovies, garlic, chives, and parsley in a blender. Blend until smooth and set aside.

Heat a sauté pan over medium-high heat and cook the bacon lardons for 5 minutes, until crispy; set aside.

Wash and dry the Castelfranco leaves, being sure to remove any excess water on the leaves. Tear the leaves into medium-size pieces and set aside.

Cook the eggs in the boiling water for 6 minutes, then shock in the ice bath. Peel the eggs and cut in half very carefully.

For each serving, toss 3 ounces Castelfranco leaves with 2 tablespoons of the dressing. Place the leaves in the middle of the salad plate and top with one-fourth each of the bacon, croutons, and avocado. Top each salad with 2 egg halves and season with sea salt and black pepper.

# BUNNY / SERVES 4
## MOROCCAN-STYLE BABY CARROT SALAD WITH CITRUS

### DRESSING

3 tablespoons extra virgin
   olive oil

2 tablespoons fresh orange
   juice

2 tablespoons fresh lemon
   juice

2 tablespoons finely minced
   shallot

1 tablespoon minced fresh
   garlic

1/4 teaspoon ground cayenne

1/4 teaspoon ground cinnamon

1 tablespoon ground cumin

Salt and freshly ground
   black pepper

1 pound mixed baby carrots

1 bunch cilantro, leaves picked

1 bunch flat-leaf parsley, leaves
   picked

1/4 cup golden raisins, chopped

1 teaspoon chile flakes

Bunny is a simple play on classic Moroccan flavors—a fresh combination of herbs, spices, and golden raisins, tailor-made to accompany grilled lamb. The carrots are not technically pickled, but their long 24-hour marinade makes them rival the flavor of the best pickled vegetables.

To make the dressing, whisk together the olive oil, orange juice, lemon juice, shallot, garlic, cayenne, cinnamon, and cumin in a small bowl. Season with salt and pepper; set aside.

Peel the baby carrots. In a bowl, toss the carrots with the dressing. Cover and let marinate in the refrigerator for 24 hours, tossing the carrots every few hours.

To serve, toss the carrots with 1/4 cup each of the cilantro and parsley leaves and place in a serving dish. Top the salad with the raisins and the chile flakes to complete.

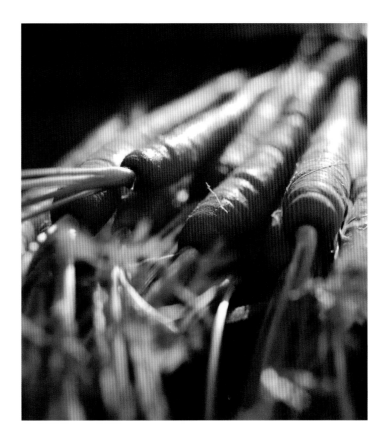

# SAN SEBASTIAN / SERVES 4
## CHORIZO AND DATES WITH GREENS

3 strips bacon, cut into lardons
($\frac{1}{2}$-inch chunks)

1 red bell pepper

2 teaspoons harissa

Salt and freshly ground
black pepper

$\frac{1}{2}$ pound chorizo, formed into
12 meatballs

$\frac{1}{4}$ cup extra virgin olive oil

2 teaspoons aged sherry
vinegar

1 bunch frisée

2 ounces mâche

4 Medjool dates, julienned

$\frac{1}{4}$ teaspoon chiffonaded basil

This dish was inspired by one of my favorite restaurants in Chicago. I think the pairing of the three main ingredients is true perfection—especially when garnished with aromatic basil and spicy chicory frisée.

---

Heat a sauté pan over medium-high heat and cook the bacon lardons for 5 minutes, until crispy. Set aside.

Over an open flame, roast the bell pepper, charring on all sides. Place in a bowl and cover with plastic wrap. When cool enough to handle, remove the skin and seeds. Place the bell pepper and harissa in a blender and purée. Season with salt and pepper. Set aside.

Heat another sauté pan over medium-high heat and sauté the meatballs until cooked through, about 5 minutes, turning them constantly. Set aside.

In a mixing bowl, whisk together the olive oil and vinegar, then season with salt and pepper. Toss the frisée and mâche with the oil and vinegar mixture.

For each serving, place 1 tablespoon of the bell pepper sauce on the plate. Arrange 3 meatballs, 1 julienned date, and 1 tablespoon bacon on the plate. Top the meatballs with about $\frac{1}{2}$ ounce of the dressed greens.

# MONTEREY / SERVES 4
## SQUID AND GIGANTE BEANS WITH CHORIZO

2 cups dried gigante beans

2 tablespoons salt

1 lemon, halved

1 red bell pepper

1/2 pound chorizo, chopped

1 pound squid, cleaned and
  sliced

Salt and freshly ground
  black pepper

1 bunch frisée

1/4 cup extra virgin olive oil

2 teaspoons fresh lemon juice

Leaves from 1 bunch chervil

1 teaspoon coarse sea salt

This simple, Spanish-style squid salad is infused with the spicy flavor of chorizo. I chose these great gigante beans for their richness and creamy texture. Seek them out at specialty food markets. If you can't find gigante beans, substitute Great Northern or Navy beans.

*Note:* If you haven't worked with squid before (and plan on having a nice evening), I highly recommend buying it already cleaned by your fishmonger and ready to cook. Between removing the beak and dealing with the squid ink mess, cleaning squid is a tricky business.

---

Soak the beans in water to cover for 4 hours. Drain. In a pot, combine the beans, 10 cups water, the salt, and the lemon halves, and simmer the beans for 1 1/2 hours. Drain and set aside. Discard the lemon halves.

While the beans are cooking, roast the bell pepper over an open flame until all sides are lightly charred. Place in a bowl and cover with plastic wrap. When cool enough to handle, remove the skin and seeds, julienne, and set aside.

Heat a large sauté pan over high heat—make sure the pan are nice and hot. Sauté the chorizo for about 1 minute, then add the squid. Cook the squid for 3 1/2 minutes, constantly flipping it. (When cooking squid, make sure that you do it at high heat for no longer than 4 minutes, or it will turn rubbery.) Add the beans and bell pepper and cook for 1 minute longer. Season with salt and pepper.

Place 8 frisée leaves on a platter and top with the sautéed squid, chorizo, and bean mixture. Drizzle with the olive oil and lemon juice. Garnish with the chervil leaves, sprinkle with the sea salt, and serve.

**130** MIXT SALADS

# PHUKET / SERVES 4
## GRILLED HANGER STEAK WITH BUCKWHEAT NOODLES

### MARINADE

1 cup red wine

1 cup teriyaki sauce

$^1/_2$ cup chopped fresh garlic

1 pound hanger steak

$^1/_2$ pound soba noodles

### DRESSING

$^1/_4$ cup toasted sesame oil

$^1/_2$ cup rice wine vinegar

1 teaspoon minced jalapeño
pepper

1 teaspoon fish sauce

2 tablespoons soy sauce

1 tablespoon minced fresh
garlic

1 tablespoon minced fresh
ginger

1 cup canola oil

Salt and freshly ground
black pepper

2 teaspoons sesame seeds
(black and white)

1 head napa cabbage, shredded

1 head green cabbage, shredded

1 large jalapeño pepper, diced

1 bunch red radishes, trimmed
and sliced

$^1/_4$ cup chopped fresh basil

1 bunch scallions, sliced

Leaves from 1 bunch
watercress

Salt and freshly ground
black pepper

Hanger steak, aka "butcher's cut," is one of my favorite cuts of meat due to its full flavor. Most of the time butchers don't like to sell this cut because they want to take it home and cook it for themselves. Good luck finding it; try not to get addicted.

To make the marinade, combine the red wine, teriyaki sauce, and garlic in a glass baking dish. Add the hanger steak and marinate, refrigerated, for 1$^1/_2$ hours.

Bring a pot of salted water to a boil on the stove. Add the soba noodles and cook for 12 minutes, or until al dente, then rinse under cold water and drain.

To make the dressing, combine the sesame oil, vinegar, jalapeño, fish sauce, soy sauce, garlic, and ginger in a blender. Slowly add the canola oil in a stream and blend until emulsified. Season with salt and pepper and set aside.

Preheat the grill to high. Season the hanger steak with salt and pepper. Grill for about 15 minutes, turning constantly. Hanger steak is a very fibrous meat, so do not cook it past medium-rare or it will become very chewy. Let the meat rest for about 4 minutes before slicing.

In a dry sauté pan over medium-high heat, toast the sesame seeds until lightly browned, about 6 minutes, watching carefully so as not to burn them.

To plate each serving, toss together 1 cup napa, 1 cup green cabbage, one-fourth of the soba, 1 tablespoon jalapeño, $^1/_4$ cup radishes, 1 tablespoon basil, 1 tablespoon scallions, $^1/_4$ cup watercress, and 3 tablespoons of the dressing. Season with salt and pepper. Top each salad with $^1/_2$ teaspoon of the toasted sesame seeds and 4 ounces sliced hanger.

# INDO
## GRAPEFRUIT AND JICAMA WITH THAI BASIL

### ROASTED PEANUTS

2 cups raw peanuts

2 teaspoons corn syrup

1/2 teaspoon ground cayenne

1 teaspoon Madras curry
powder

2 tablespoons sugar

1 teaspoon salt

Pinch of freshly ground
black pepper


4 cups shredded red cabbage


### DRESSING

1/2 cup fresh orange juice

1/2 cup rice wine vinegar

2 teaspoons sugar

1/2 teaspoon chopped fresh
garlic

1 tablespoon chopped fresh
ginger

1 tablespoon chopped Thai
basil

1 cup canola oil

Salt and freshly ground
black pepper


1 pound jicama, julienned

1 grapefruit, peeled, seeded,
and sliced

4 teaspoons chiffonaded mint

1/4 cup fresh cilantro leaves

Salt and freshly ground
black pepper

This refreshing marriage of flavors from Asia and Mexico is sure to brighten up any winter day. If you're a fan of the Siam at Mixt Greens, think of this as an amped version of that salad—with more complex flavors and a wider variety of textures, it's on another level.

---

Preheat the oven to 350°F.

To prepare the peanuts, combine the peanuts, corn syrup, cayenne, curry powder, sugar, salt, pepper, and 1/2 teaspoon water in a bowl. Spread on a baking sheet and roast for 15 minutes. Let cool, then coarsely chop.

While the peanuts are cooking, rinse the shredded cabbage under cold water to let the color bleed out. Dry the cabbage with paper towels.

To make the dressing, combine the orange juice, vinegar, sugar, garlic, ginger, and Thai basil in a blender. Slowly add the oil in a stream and blend until emulsified. Season with salt and pepper and set aside.

To plate each serving, toss 1 cup cabbage, one-fourth of the julienned jicama, one-fourth of the grapefruit slices, 1 teaspoon mint, and 1 tablespoon cilantro with 2 1/2 tablespoons of the dressing. Season with salt and pepper and garnish each salad with 2 tablespoons of the roasted peanuts.

# PASSION / SERVES 4
## CRAB AND CITRUS WITH PASSION FRUIT

**DRESSING**

¹/₄ cup fresh orange juice

2 tablespoons champagne vinegar

2 tablespoons passion fruit purée

1 tablespoon agave nectar

Salt and freshly ground black pepper

2 heads butter lettuce

¹/₂ pound fresh crabmeat

1 bunch chives, chopped

1 bunch red radishes, sliced

2 avocados, peeled, seeded, and sliced

2 Cara Cara oranges, peeled and sliced

1 grapefruit, peeled, seeded, and sliced

Salt and freshly ground black pepper

Here, I was interested in mixing the freshness of the sea—to me that means crab—with an exotic fruit combination. To that end, the bright flavors of winter citrus mixed with one of South America's tropical jewels, passion fruit, was a no-brainer for me. The flavors hit on salty, rich, and acidic notes; don't pass this one over.

To make the dressing, place the orange juice, vinegar, passion fruit, and agave nectar in a blender and blend until incorporated. Season with salt and pepper.

Remove the outside leaves of the lettuce, then separate the remaining leaves. Squeeze any excess water out of the crabmeat.

For each serving, combine the leaves from half of a head of lettuce with 1 tablespoon chives, 10 radish slices, 6 avocado slices, 8 orange slices, and 6 grapefruit slices. Toss gently with 1¹/₂ tablespoons of the dressing and season with salt and pepper. Arrange on a plate and top with one-fourth of the crabmeat.

# BISTRO / SERVES 4
## FILET OF BEEF WITH PROPER FIXINGS

**DRESSING**

1/2 cup red wine vinegar

1 tablespoon Dijon mustard

1 tablespoon minced fresh garlic

1/2 teaspoon Tabasco sauce

1/2 teaspoon Worcestershire sauce

1 cup extra virgin olive oil

Salt and freshly ground black pepper

4 (4-ounce) beef filets

Salt and freshly ground black pepper

2 hearts romaine, shredded

4 tablespoons capers, drained

4 tablespoons finely diced shallot

4 tablespoons sliced cornichon

4 tablespoons sliced red radish

Leaves from 1 bunch tarragon

4 tablespoons brioche bread crumbs

4 quail eggs

This is my salad version of the classic, featuring seared beef tenderloin and completed with all of the traditional accompaniments.

---

Preheat the grill to high.

To make the dressing, combine the vinegar, mustard, garlic, Tabasco, and Worcestershire in a blender. Slowly add the olive oil in a stream and blend until emulsified. Season with salt and pepper and set aside.

Season the beef on both sides with salt and pepper and grill for 4 minutes per side, to rare. Let the meat rest for 2 minutes, then cut into a small dice.

For each serving, place one-fourth of a sliced heart of romaine in the bowl. Add 1 tablespoon capers, 1 tablespoon shallot, 1 tablespoon cornichon, 1 tablespoon radish, and 8 tarragon leaves and toss with 1 tablespoon of the dressing. Top with 1 tablespoon bread crumbs. Place 1 whole diced filet on top and crack 1 quail egg over the top of each one. Give it a good toss.

# TROPICAL / SERVES 4
## MIXED CITRUS AND FRESH COCONUT

1 grapefruit

2 Cara Cara oranges

2 blood oranges

1 jicama

1 pineapple, peeled, cored, and diced

2 tablespoons chiffonaded fresh basil leaves

Grated fresh coconut for garnish

Tropical is my modern version of ambrosia salad—minus the marshmallows and mayonnaise, of course. If you're not familiar with Cara Cara oranges, their taste is a cross between a grapefruit and an orange—a true gem during cold winter months.

---

Peel the grapefruit and all the oranges. Slice the grapefruit and oranges into rounds or whole moons. Make sure you cut the citrus types separately from one another, because their juices are different colors and they will bleed into each other. Peel and cut the jicama into a small dice.

Arrange the citrus on a large serving plate or individual serving plates, then top with the pineapple, jicama, and basil. Garnish with the freshly grated coconut and serve.

# EGGHEAD / SERVES 4
## FARM EGG WITH CAVIAR AND POACHED QUAIL EGG

8 organic farm eggs

2 heads butter lettuce

2 tablespoons mayonnaise

1 tablespoon finely diced
    shallot

1 teaspoon Dijon mustard

2 tablespoons finely diced
    cornichon

Sea salt and freshly ground
    black pepper

$1/2$ teaspoon white vinegar

8 quail eggs

2 tablespoons caviar (Surgeon
    royal)

1 bunch of chives, tips only

This is the Rolls Royce of egg salad: a luxurious finger food. The combination of the warm, rich quail egg yolk and the salty-rich caviar is nothing short of pure decadence.

---

Bring a pot of water to a boil on the stove. Prepare a bowl of ice water.

Boil the farm eggs for 12 minutes, then shock them in the ice bath.

While the eggs are cooling, carefully peel off the large, outer leaves of the lettuce and set 8 of them aside—these will be your lettuce cups for serving the salad.

Peel the farm eggs, cut them into quarters, and slice. In a bowl, combine the eggs, mayonnaise, shallot, mustard, and cornichon. Season with salt and pepper.

Bring a small pot of water and the vinegar to a simmer on the stove. Carefully break the quail eggs and add to the water 1 at a time. Poach the quail eggs for about 2 minutes, depending on the size of your quail eggs.

Scoop the egg salad into each of the 8 lettuce cups. Place 1 quail egg on top of the egg salad, add a dollop of caviar, then top with one chive tip. Place 2 lettuce cups on each of 4 plates and serve.

# CLASSIC / SERVES 4
## HEARTS OF ROMAINE WITH MINI CROUTONS

### CROUTONS

1 sweet roll

2 tablespoons extra virgin
   olive oil

Salt and freshly ground
   black pepper

### DRESSING

$1/2$ cup mayonnaise

2 tablespoons champagne
   vinegar

1 teaspoon minced fresh garlic

2 teaspoons fresh lemon juice

1 teaspoon Dijon mustard

4 salt-packed anchovies

$1/2$ cup freshly grated
   Parmesan cheese

$1/2$ cup grapeseed oil

Salt and freshly ground
   black pepper

2 hearts romaine

Sea salt and freshly ground
   black pepper

8 white Spanish anchovy fillets

I've come up with a simple idea to enhance everyone's Caesar salad experience: the mini crouton. No longer will your mouth be cut while eating monster croutons, and you will enjoy the crouton flavor in every single bite. Go mini croutons!

---

Preheat the oven to 375°F.

To make the croutons, cut the sweet roll into small cubes about $1/4$-inch square. Place 1 cup of the bread cubes in a mixing bowl and toss with the olive oil. Season with salt and pepper. Spread on a baking sheet and toast in the oven for 10 minutes, or until golden brown. Set aside.

To make the dressing, combine the mayonnaise, vinegar, garlic, lemon juice, mustard, anchovies, and Parmesan in a blender. Slowly add the oil in a stream and blend until emulsified. Season with salt and pepper and set aside.

Cut off the bottom of each romaine heart, carefully pull apart the leaves, and rinse under cold water. Remove all excess water from the leaves.

For each serving, stack 5 leaves in the middle of the plate and drizzle with 2 tablespoons of the dressing. Top with the mini croutons and season with sea salt and pepper. Place 1 anchovy fillet on either side of the romaine leaves.

# CAPTIVA / SERVES 4
## BUTTER LETTUCE WITH CITRUS AND AVOCADO

**PICKLED ONION**

1 cup cider vinegar

1 cup fresh lime juice

1 jalapeño pepper, chopped

1 tablespoon sugar

1 red onion, thinly sliced

**DRESSING**

3 tablespoons fresh Meyer
    lemon juice

1 tablespoon champagne
    vinegar

1 teaspoon agave nectar

3 tablespoons extra virgin
    olive oil

Salt and freshly ground
    black pepper

2 heads butter lettuce, leaves
    washed and removed

2 avocados, peeled, seeded, and
    sliced

2 grapefruits, peeled and sliced

Salt and freshly ground
    black pepper

$1/_2$ cup chopped macadamia
    nuts, for garnish

Here's another recipe I developed on the spot while hanging out in Captiva last winter. It's perfect beach food because it's light and healthy and won't mess up your beach bod.

To make the pickled onion, combine the vinegar, lime juice, jalapeño, sugar, and onions in a bowl. Let marinate for 2 hours at room temperature.

To make the dressing, combine the lemon juice, vinegar, and agave in a blender. Slowly add the olive oil in a stream and blend to emulsify. Season with salt and pepper, and set aside.

To plate each serving, toss half of a lettuce head with half of an avocado, half of a grapefruit, 2 tablespoons of the pickled onion, and 1 tablespoon of the dressing. Season with salt and pepper and garnish with 2 tablespoons macadamia nuts.

# CRUDO / SERVES 4
## ARCTIC CHAR WITH FRESH HORSERADISH

**HORSERADISH CREAM**

8 tablespoons crème fraîche

2 tablespoons freshly grated
   horseradish

Salt and freshly ground black
   pepper


1 pound arctic char, cleaned

1 bulb fennel, thinly shaved,
   fronds reserved for garnish

4 Cara Cara oranges, peeled
   and sliced

1/4 cup extra virgin olive oil

2 tablespoons fresh lemon
   juice

Salt and freshly ground
   black pepper

1 bunch chives, chopped, for
   garnish

I've chosen to use arctic char here for its firm texture and delicate flavor. It's a sustainable farmed fish choice, so please use it as a substitute for farmed salmon.

To make the horseradish cream, combine the crème fraîche and horseradish in a small bowl and season with salt and pepper. Let sit for one hour.

Cut the char into 16 slices.

For each serving, toss 1/4 cup shaved fennel and 1 sliced orange with 1 tablespoon olive oil and 1/2 tablespoon lemon juice in a bowl. Season with salt and pepper. Place 2 tablespoons of the horseradish cream on a plate, and add 4 slices of fish on top of the cream. Top with the fennel and orange mixture and garnish with the chives and a few fennel fronds.

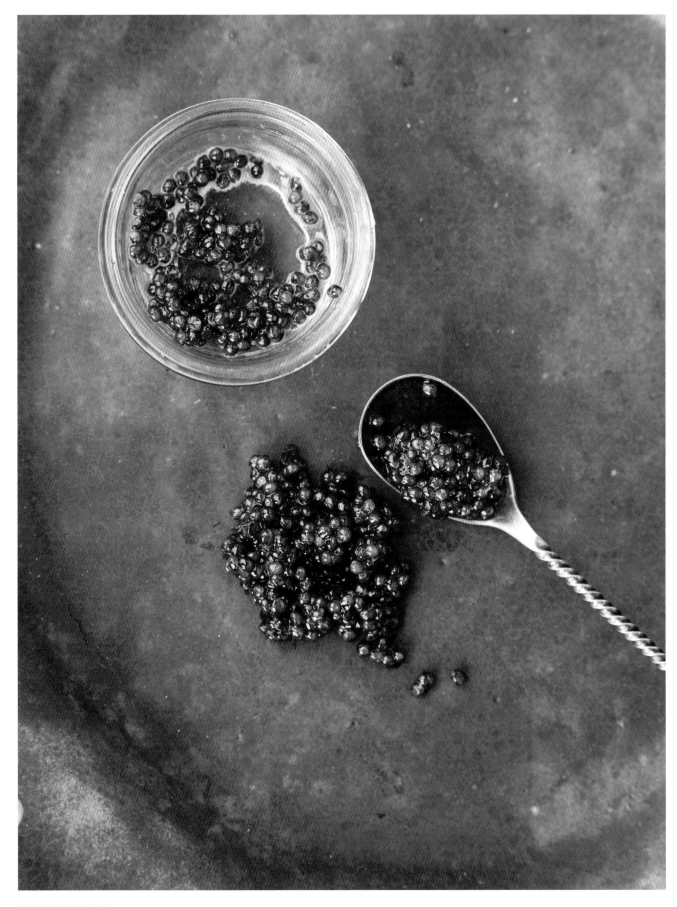

# TOWER / SERVES 4
## TUNA TARTARE

### YUZU SAUCE

1 teaspoon yuzu juice

$1/4$ teaspoon white soy sauce

2 teaspoons unseasoned rice wine vinegar

$1/4$ cup mayonnaise

### TUNA

1 pound ahi (sushi grade), finely diced

2 tablespoons plus 2 teaspoons sesame oil

2 teaspoons minced fresh garlic

2 teaspoons minced fresh ginger

1 tablespoon plus 1 teaspoon minced jalapeño pepper

Salt and freshly ground black pepper

6 tablespoons chopped avocado

$1/2$ cup peeled, seeded, and chopped into small dice cucumber

4 teaspoons caviar (Sturgeon royal)

Plain and simple, this is my take on tartare. It's the straight-up philosophy of how I make food, with a variety of textures and flavors. There's the saltiness of the caviar, the clean ocean taste of the tuna, the acid from the yuzu, and the creaminess of the avocado, finished with the crunch of cucumber. This should please any foodie who dines at your table.

---

To make the yuzu sauce, whisk together the yuzu, soy sauce, rice wine vinegar, and mayonnaise in a bowl; set aside.

To make the tuna, toss together the ahi, sesame oil, garlic, ginger, and jalapeño in another bowl. Season with salt and pepper.

To serve, place $1^{1}/_{2}$ teaspoons of the yuzu sauce in the center of each plate. Place a $2^{1}/_{2}$-inch ring mold in the center of the plate. Layer the ingredients, starting with the avocado, then the cucumber, then the tuna. Top each with 1 teaspoon caviar.

# TREAT / SERVES 4
## ROASTED FINGERLING POTATOES WITH HERBS AND TRUFFLE CHEESE

1½ pounds mixed fingerling
potatoes

2 tablespoons extra virgin
olive oil

Sea salt and freshly ground
black pepper

1 teaspoon chopped fresh
flat-leaf parsley

½ teaspoon chopped fresh
thyme

½ teaspoon chopped fresh
oregano

½ pound *tartufo moliterno*,
(or other raw sheep's milk
truffle cheese)

I came up with this earthy combination to be served alongside a big hunk of juicy rib-eye. I added my favorite truffle cheese for pure decadence and enjoyment; grate as much as you want on top, indulge yourself. Go truffles! You can find truffle cheese at Whole Foods and specialty shops.

---

Preheat the oven to 375°F.

Cut each of the potatoes in half and place in a bowl. Toss with the olive oil and season with a pinch of salt and pepper. Spread on a baking sheet and roast in the oven for 25 minutes, or until lightly golden brown. Let cool for a few minutes.

Place the potatoes on a serving platter. Top with the chopped fresh herbs and season with sea salt and black pepper. Grate the desired amount of truffle cheese over the top and serve.

# INDEX

# THANKS . . .

To Leslie and Dave, thanks for all the support over the years, and for helping me turn my dreams into a reality.

To Joanne, I couldn't have done this without you.

To Meme, thanks for being the greatest grandmother in the world.

To Wendy, thanks for all the encouragement and caring that you have given me over the years.

To Barbra, thanks for "investing" in me.

Katie, thanks for all your help with the recipe testing. You rock!

To Tony and Matt, thanks for your dedication and all your hard work.

To the MC staff, the greatest employees on the planet, thank you for keeping my vision alive. Keep up the good work.